ISBN 978-0-9575584-6-5
© Copyright 2018
Pack Leader Publications
All rights reserved

Accelerate school improvement through authentic self-evaluation

www.keep-soaring.com

How to navigate Keep Soaring

Who Keep Soaring is for 1
Why you need Keep Soaring 1
The purpose of Keep Soaring 2
What Keep Soaring means… 3
How Keep Soaring is organised 4
How to get the best from Keep Soaring 5
Some terms used in Keep Soaring 6

CHAPTER 1: INTRODUCTION
Background and research 7
Purpose of self-evaluation 10
Process of self-evaluation 11
People and self-evaluation 12
Strategy for self-evaluation 13

CHAPTER 2: PURPOSE
What is self-evaluation? 15
Why self-evaluate? 15
Problems of self-evaluation 16
Starting points 18
Focal points 22
Pin points 26
Pressure points 30

The right setting for self-evaluation 34
Levels of self-evaluation 45
Means end self-evaluation 46
Awareness Reflection Responsibility Action 47

CHAPTER 3: PROCESS
Agreeing the context for self-evaluation 55
Methodology of self-evaluation 62
Impact 64
Evaluation trails 67
Collecting evidence 73
Scheduling self-evaluation 75
Speed of self-evaluation 78
Awareness Reflection Responsibility Action 83

CHAPTER 4: PEOPLE
Roles and self-evaluation 91
Responsibilities 93
Expectations 93
Boundaries 93
The principal 94
Senior and middle leaders 94
Language of self-evaluation 96

Quantifiers 98
Technicals 99
Descriptors 100
Giving self-evaluation a voice 101
How people behave towards self-evaluation ... 104
Planning and approach 105
Evidence and rigour 108
Resources and allocation 110
Awareness Reflection Responsibility Action 113

CHAPTER 5: KEEP SOARING
Strategy and all things strategic 121
Get off the train 122
Get out of the balloon 123
Get into the helicopter 124
Keep Soaring 125
Developing your strategy 126
Strategy for self-evaluation 127
Flight plan 130
Authentic evidence-based school-led 131

AUTHORS 133
FURTHER READING 135

Who Keep Soaring is for

It is tempting to suggest that this book is written for all stakeholders in your school, since they all should be actively involved in self-evaluation, however the main intended reader is the school's most senior leader. We recognise that different schools have different staffing structures and job titles so, from now on, we will refer to the main reader as 'principal' although your actual position or professional title may be different.

Why you need Keep Soaring

Regardless of whether you are an established principal with years of service under your belt or a new principal, where reality has suddenly kicked in, you are expected to have your finger on the pulse of your school. In order to do this, you need to be able to engage and support all stakeholders without taking on the burden of doing everything yourself. This can be an overwhelming challenge that places multiple competing demands on your time (and sanity) and can leave you in a very isolated and sometimes vulnerable position. No two days are the same because schools are living, breathing, dynamic organisations where everyone should be constantly pushing the boundaries of their own learning but, be under no illusions, the buck stops with you.

You will quickly find that this book contains important messages for other stakeholders, so please don't keep it to yourself; connect with your colleagues, start a conversation, share your reflections and ideas. Everyone has a vital role to play in successful self-evaluation and, to be **authentic**, it has to be led by your individual school's specific needs and context.

The purpose of Keep Soaring

Keep Soaring is designed to get to the heart of what really matters to drive and **accelerate improvement** in your school.

We believe that school self-evaluation is the one and only **strategy** for continuous improvement in your school that aligns all your processes and people with purpose to demonstrate impact on student and staff learning and outcomes. It is the essential core of any school but too many schools now self-evaluate for the wrong reasons. In our experience, self-evaluation has been allowed to grow to a point where it is a cumbersome process that takes huge amounts of professional time, energy and resources without always delivering a commensurate return on this investment. This is because it is typically a response to external demands such as inspection or accreditation and validation visits.

The purpose of Keep Soaring is to help you develop a clear strategy that makes sure your self-evaluation is framed by the leadership decisions you have taken (**school-led**) and drives the right activities to collect the right evidence (**evidence-based**) to put the learning of your students in your school at the heart of everything you do (**authentic**).

We want to help you to challenge your current practice and identify what you are doing and why you are doing it. Only then can you step back and truly evaluate how all your planning and monitoring efforts are working in the school and identify which ones are genuinely contributing to improvements in student outcomes. Once you know this, you can strip away the layers of unnecessary activity and put renewed focus on all stakeholders working together to accelerate improvement.

What Keep Soaring means

Keep Soaring is the metaphor for the process we will use to support your personal reflection as you develop your school's strategy for self-evaluation. We will help you move from a linear inflexible approach (train) to a more rounded reflective view (balloon) and ultimately guide you to produce a strategy (flight plan) based on a responsive three-dimensional helicopter view of your school and its performance.

Get off the train

Get out of the balloon

Get into the helicopter

How Keep Soaring is organised

Keep Soaring is structured into five chapters – each with a specific focus.

① Introduction — This chapter explains the theory and background to school effectiveness, school improvement and self-evaluation, and draws on academic research to highlight the issues facing schools.

② Purpose — This chapter guides you through the key purpose of self-evaluation and encourages you to reflect on the purpose of self-evaluation in your own school.

③ Process — This chapter guides you through the different elements of the self-evaluation process and encourages you to reflect on scheduling, speed and the 'how' of self-evaluation in your own school.

④ People — This chapter guides you through the different people that should be contributing to self-evaluation and encourages you to reflect on the role and accountability of different stakeholders in your own school.

⑤ Keep Soaring — This section consolidates your learning by creating a strategy (flight plan) for self-evaluation in your own school.

How to get the best from Keep Soaring

The temptation is often to skip the introductory chapters and jump to the solutions but, to get the best from your experience, we recommend working through the book sequentially as different sections are deliberately designed to build on previous content and reflection. The intention behind each chapter is to raise awareness, prompt reflection and increase responsibility thereby leading to action that is authentic because it is defined by the school.

Chapter 1 provides an introduction to the topic of self-evaluation and draws on a range of research and practical experience. Chapters 2, 3 and 4 present the Purpose, Process and People related to authentic self-evaluation. Each of these chapters is presented in a standard format and contains some key questions and activities intended to raise your awareness and prompt reflection around the current situation in your school. At the end of each chapter you will have some decisions to make around responsibility and future action, which should be recorded for later use.

Chapter 5 summarises the Keep Soaring flight plan approach to develop your school's **strategy for self-evaluation**, drawing on the outcomes from the previous chapters. It provides a blueprint to communicate your school's alignment of the 3Ps to accelerate improvement and demonstrate impact.

Some terms used in Keep Soaring

Self-evaluation applies to any school, regardless of the school's structure and designation, geographical location, the age range of students or the curriculum being taught. There are, however, some variations in the vocabulary and terminology used by different schools and we have therefore defined the meaning of some terms that we will use throughout this book.

Principal	The most senior leader in the school.
Leaders	Any other leader in the school.
Cohort	A group of students (can be categorised by age, gender, language, need, etc.).
Year/Grade	A cohort of students organised by age into a coherent teaching group.
Operational	An outline of what you will focus on for the near future, with details of activity, timescales and measurement of results.
Strategic	An outline of your mission, vision, high-level goals, and the projects required to achieve these, for the next 3-5 years.
Strategy	A blueprint for achieving success over a period of time, with a clearly defined purpose and outcomes.

INTRODUCTION

CHAPTER 1

Background and research

School improvement, school effectiveness and school self-evaluation are terms that are regularly used in educational circles around the world … but what do they really mean and how should they integrate and complement each other to promote a higher quality of education for students?

Extensive research around **school effectiveness** has focused on exploring differences between schools that are judged to be more or less effective based on their educational performance, which is usually defined through benchmarked metrics and quantitative measures on the basis of examination results. In contrast, **school improvement** research has concentrated more on the actual processes and tools that schools have used to improve outcomes, and have therefore become associated with changes that are often evidenced using a broader range of in-school data. In other words, school effectiveness is more about the operation and performance of a school as an organisation (viewed from an external perspective) while school improvement is about changes in the internal workings of the school that will ultimately improve its effectiveness. Examples of school improvement are usually reported as case studies illustrating the changes in processes, systems and provision that have brought about improvement in individual or groups of schools.

We believe that the capacity for a school to improve its effectiveness hinges on the quality of the leadership and management decisions taken and the consistency, rigour and commitment with which these decisions are implemented through a culture of change, learning and continuous development by all stakeholders. Taking difficult decisions, planning for short, medium and long-term development, and putting new initiatives into practice are only part of the picture. A school can have all of this in place but will still need a way to measure and evaluate the impact of the original decisions and the subsequent actions that had been taken. **Self-evaluation** should be seen as a strategy that is led by the internal leadership decisions in a school. It should focus specifically on the impact of the school's planning and implementation of these decisions, evidenced and measured by the outcomes of the students in the school.

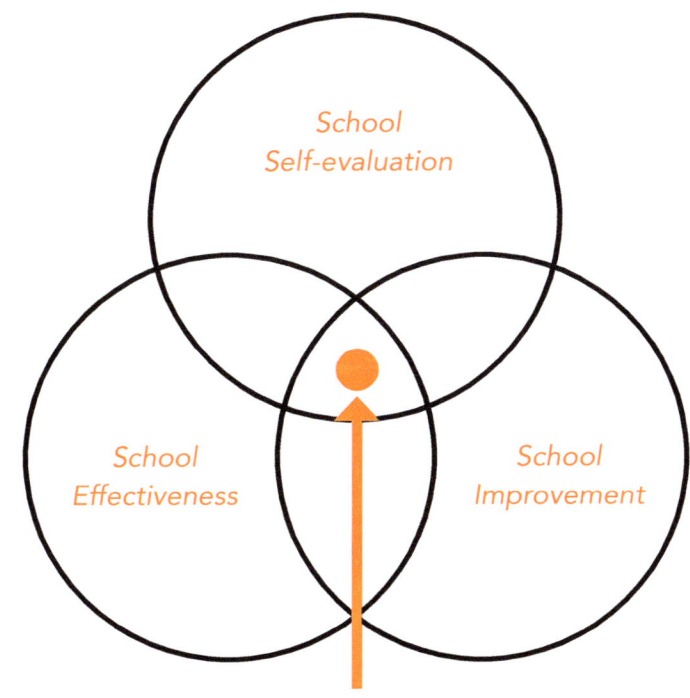

How does your school self-evaluation measure the impact of your school improvement decisions and planning in relation to the impact on your school's effectiveness?

A review of educational research and literature shows that the three components of school effectiveness, school improvement and school self-evaluation are often considered separately, causing a disjointed and fragmented approach to overall improvement. We believe that if a school implements authentic, evidence-based, school-led self-evaluation, then this will have a positive impact and demonstrate improvement that in turn increases the school's effectiveness. To achieve this, a school needs to define a clear **strategy** for its self-evaluation.

A critical appraisal of the literature on the impact and authenticity of school self-evaluation research over the past 15 years shows that this is still a relatively new and evolving area of study. However, a number of common themes and core messages are already emerging and support our view that schools need to develop a strategy for their self-evaluation to ensure that it is purposeful, evidence-based and school-led rather than simply a quality assurance process driven by inspection and other external meta-evaluation processes.

The concept behind Keep Soaring is to raise your awareness and prompt reflection about what really matters in your school. Once identified, you are in a better position to take responsibility for future action on the basis of your self-evaluation and determine whether these decisions have made a difference. To do this, you will need to step back from the detail of daily routines – we suggest getting into your helicopter – and demonstrate an impact by collecting quality assured evidence that aligns with the purpose, process and people in your school. You will only see the integration of purpose, process and people if you rise above the detail and have a strategy for self-evaluation.

Purpose
Understand **why** you are doing self-evaluation and what you are trying to achieve in the school.

Process
Recognise **what** activities are being carried out in the school and **how** they contribute to self-evaluation.

People
Recognise **who** is involved and understand how people are behaving in relation to self-evaluation in the school.

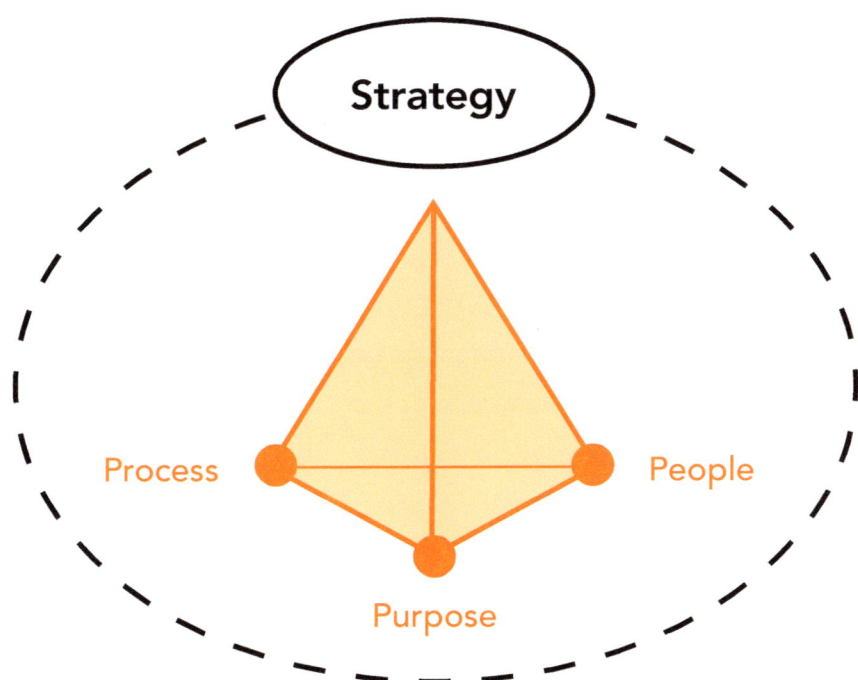

Purpose of self-evaluation

Self-evaluation is not a new concept for schools. However, research indicates that both the context and audience for self-evaluation have changed significantly over the years and are heavily dependent on the country where the self-evaluation is being implemented and the regulatory requirements for schools in that geographical location. Much of the research focuses on self-evaluation as an internal school improvement tool – part of the heart of the school – but also acknowledges that it is often perceived as a 'bolt on' series of activities that can take over from other important activities and functions in the school. In these instances, teachers' participation and ownership in the process are often diminished resulting in negative perceptions.

The reliability and impact of school self-evaluation is a topic that has been heavily scrutinised and has given rise to a range of issues and concerns. For example, a number of studies have questioned the in-school variability of teachers and leaders (at all levels) to accurately evaluate a school's weaknesses. This has been attributed to a number of reasons, such as a lack of evaluative capacity, a lack of technical and data analysis skills, and the mindset of staff. The challenge that is emerging is for schools to embed self-evaluation into their professional culture in such a way as to make it part of daily practice, but with a clarity of purpose and precision that establishes a meaningful process for all members of the school community.

Process of self-evaluation

There are many definitions of self-evaluation as a process and they all have similarities based around reflection on practice and the collection of a range of data from diverse sources. Most definitions suggest that self-evaluation is a set of structures and systematic processes that are conducted within a coherent framework. However, there is no universal framework available to underpin self-evaluation and this is typically one of the challenges faced by schools. Consequently, one approach that many schools have adopted is to develop models and best practice based on what has worked in other schools, and particularly in 'outstanding' schools. Although there is always something to learn from sharing best practice, and schools do have many common processes and activities, this is a questionable approach because it suggests that there is a potential one-size fits all solution to self-evaluation. The fundamental principle of self-evaluation is the **self** aspect, which must be tailored specifically to the context and needs of each individual school at all times. This will require schools to develop their own strategy for self-evaluation and then to consider the processes and people that align best with what they are trying to achieve (purpose).

The research agenda appears to be shifting away from the early concepts of self-evaluation (as a process) validated externally and moving to the consideration of the impact and outcomes of improvement driven, intelligent accountability of schools. In other words, schools are being challenged to look at their internal processes and roles of stakeholders to determine how these can be used to stimulate improvement in the areas of student outcomes and professional learning. This shift is being driven, in part, by the realisation that the power and potential of true self-evaluation is not being realised. The current reality is that self-evaluation driven by external factors is more likely to produce negative attitudes and stress among school staff.

People and self-evaluation

The move to intelligent accountability of the key stakeholders in schools has highlighted the moral imperative of school leaders to accept responsibility as agents of change and to be held to account for developing self-improving systems in their schools. As learning organisations, schools are being urged to go further and develop their professional capital and culture by engaging teachers and students in self-evaluation at grassroots level.

The role and responsibility of the school principal is paramount in ensuring that key systems in the school are effective and that the key system leaders understand their own strengths and weaknesses. Where schools have demonstrated rapid improvement, research has highlighted the growing significance of ensuring and developing the effectiveness of the principal across a range of systems, including:

- Driving improvement planning
- Providing strategic leadership
- Engaging distributed leadership
- Improving the quality of teaching and learning outcomes
- Securing parental confidence

These expectations on a principal transcend a school's structure, organisation and curriculum and it is unlikely that any principal would dispute or argue against any of them. However, the bigger expectation is that a principal should lead and manage the integral connections between leadership, learning and self-evaluation to provide a robust and reliable outcome. Too often, national inspection findings and research studies report that bias and self-delusion exist with the result that school self-evaluation presents an overly positive interpretation of the quality of teaching and learning. This brings a specific challenge for principals – to ensure that your people are confident and competent to make accurate evaluative judgements.

Strategy for self-evaluation

Most studies conclude that both internal (self-evaluation) and external evaluations (inspections/peer reviews) of schools are required to stimulate school improvement and hold schools accountable for their effectiveness. The cost of national inspections is becoming too burdensome and attempts are being made to decentralise schools from government control in many countries. Increasingly, robust self-evaluation at individual school level is becoming one of the defining measures for both leadership and overall school performance judgements. This has led to increased pressure on school leaders to manage school autonomy and to accept responsibility for the quality of teaching (provision) and learning (outcomes) in their own school.

It is widely accepted that rigorous, robust and systematic self-evaluation is necessary to drive successful improvement in any school. Authentic evidence-based school-led self-evaluation is the core strategy for continuous improvement in the areas that matter most to each individual school. To achieve this, school leaders need to start thinking differently about self-evaluation and school improvement. Start by challenging what you do, why you are doing it, and what is changing (improving) as a result of all the time, energy and effort that is currently being invested into self-evaluation.

Then connect the dots between the leadership decisions that have been taken and the impact you expect these decisions to have on students' learning.

By stepping back and bringing inter-connectivity to existing school systems and processes, it is possible to simplify what you do and increase your school's effectiveness at the same time. To do this, you will need a blueprint for self-evaluation that is evidence-based and led by decisions in your school – this is your Keep Soaring Strategy.

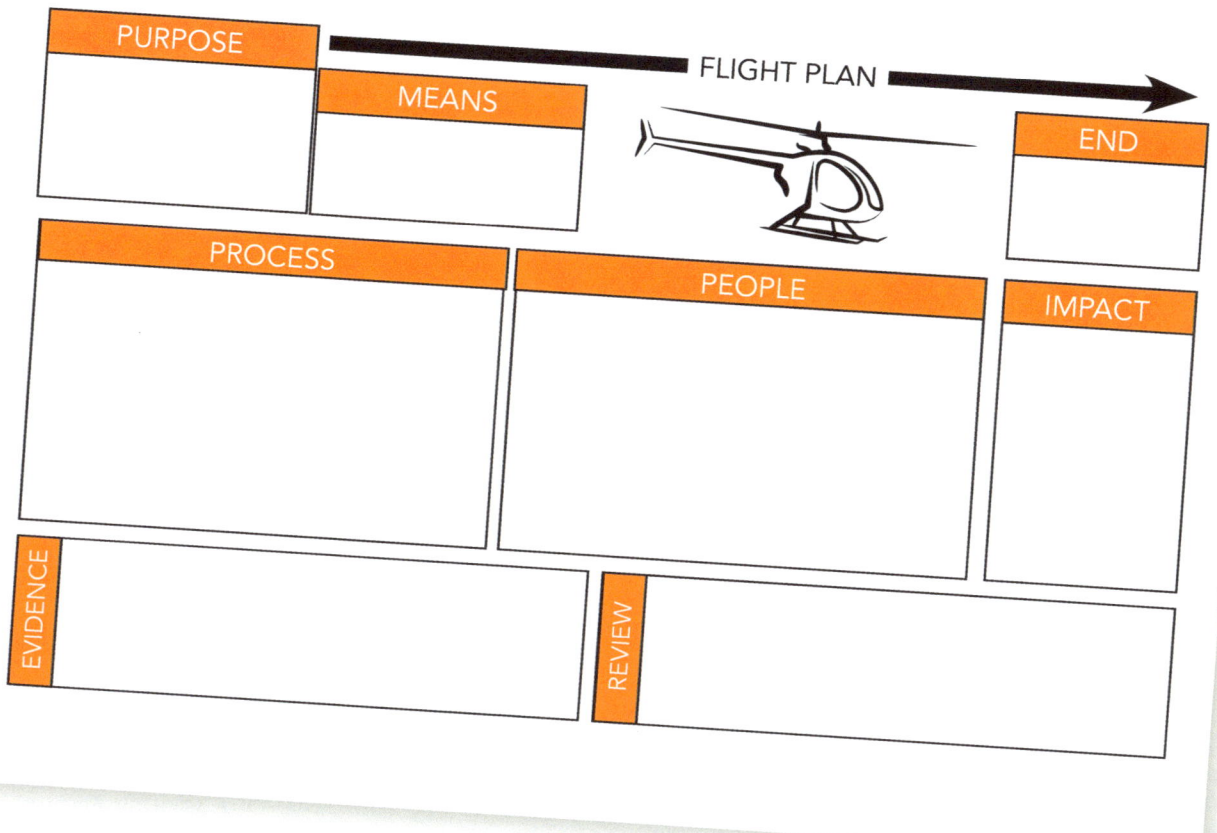

The next three chapters focus on the **purpose**, **process** and **people** involved in your school's self-evaluation. The key questions and activities in each chapter are designed to raise your self-awareness and encourage self-reflection, leading to responsibility for action, which should build your Keep Soaring Strategy as you progress through the rest of the book.

CHAPTER
2

PURPOSE

What is self-evaluation?

Self-evaluation is the fundamental core of any school improvement process. However, in recent years, the term 'self-evaluation' is becoming synonymous with inspection, audit and accreditation for too many people. As a result, the power and potential of true self-evaluation is often lost in translation, especially when used as a management tool rather than a driver for strategic thinking and action.

Why self-evaluate?

Self-evaluation is necessary to drive successful improvement in any school.

It is not a one-off event driven by inspection or external accreditation and validation. It should be the core ingredient of continuous improvement and involve all stakeholders, where the teachers and school leaders are the key drivers and agents of change.

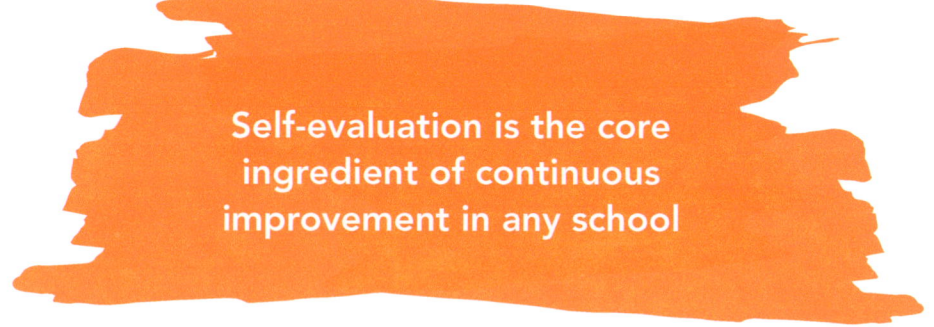

Self-evaluation is the core ingredient of continuous improvement in any school

15

Problems of self-evaluation

Self-evaluation doesn't work as well as it should if it is driven purely by factors outside the school. External influences, such as inspection or accreditation and validation, provide a framework for self-evaluation but they are driven by a centralised strategy that takes no account of the school's unique context. The purpose of self-evaluation is to provide an ongoing mechanism for making improvements over an academic year based on the leadership decisions that are relevant and appropriate at the time. It is therefore important to take positive advantage of every day, every week, every month in the life of the school year because the academic year has its own natural pulse and rhythm that must be built into your self-evaluation process and schedule. The speed at which you will be able to accelerate school improvement very much depends on how well you connect the dots between the core elements of purpose, process and people.

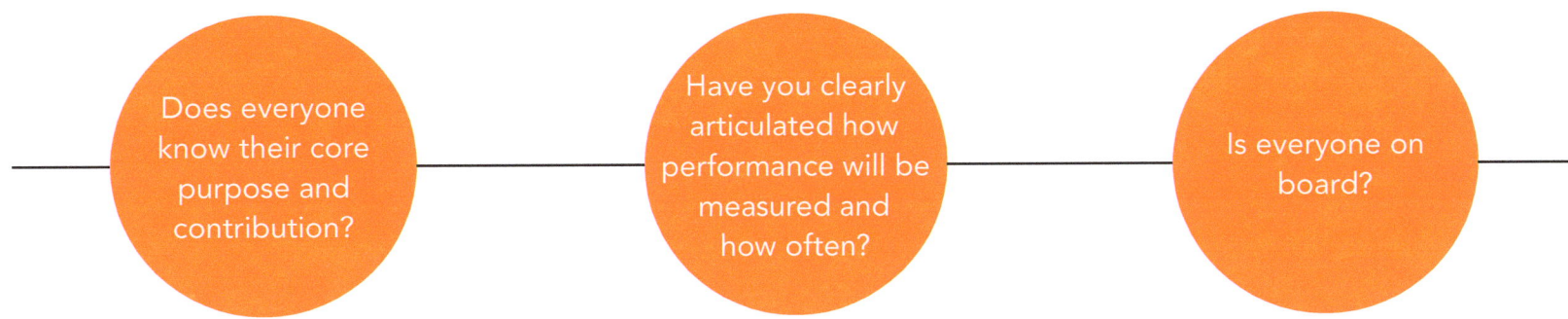

Let's look at some of the most obvious problems of self-evaluation in schools. Once you identify the stumbling block or blockage in your own school, then you are better adept at turning the problem into an opportunity for improvement and development.

Examine which points need more attention so that you can develop an evidence-based school-led **strategy** and **accelerate** your school's progress.

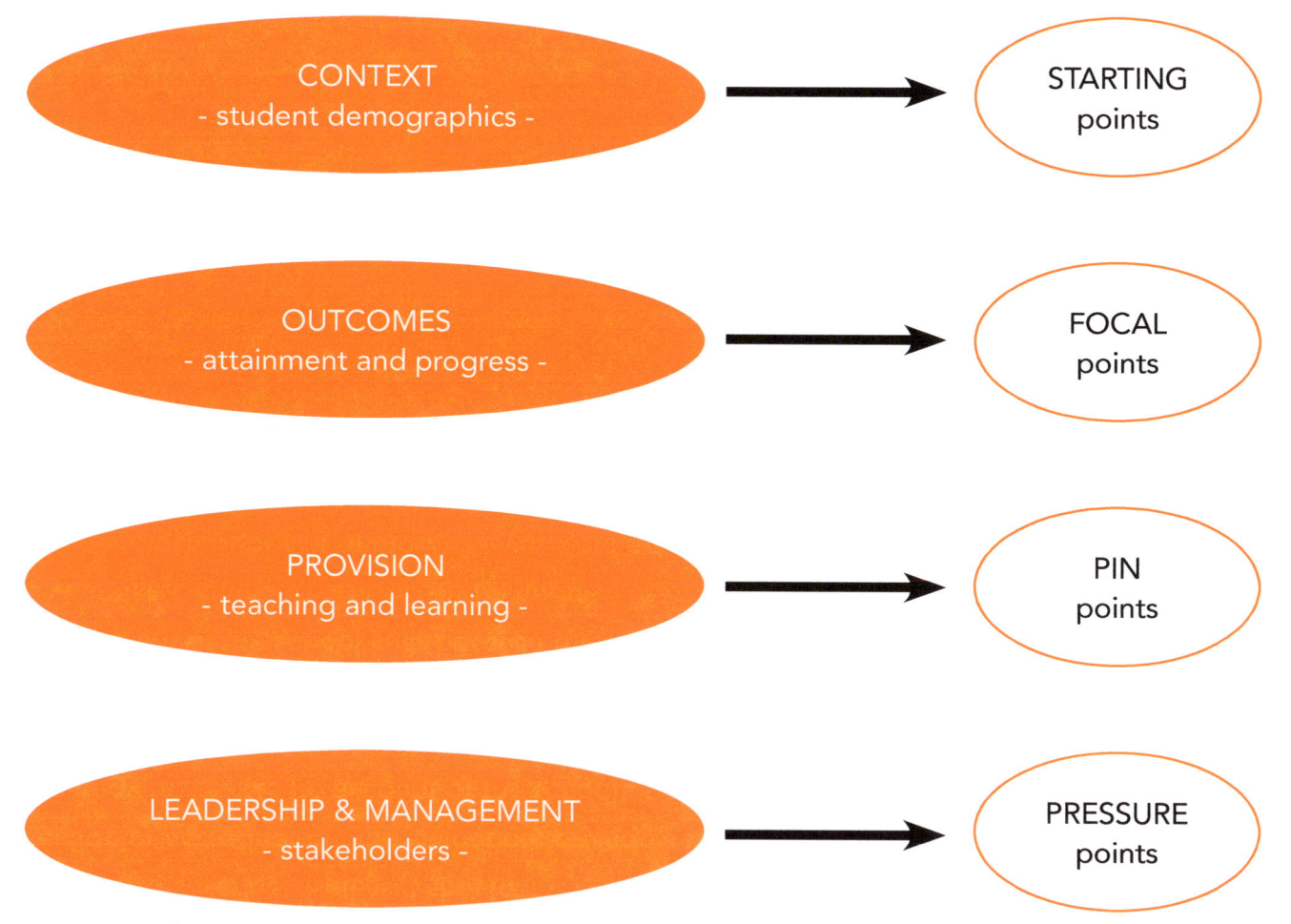

Starting points

Every school is different – no two are the same. Schools that follow the same curriculum and belong to the same cluster of schools may appear similar, but a school's context is defined by a combination of factors including the unique and individual characteristics of the students within the school community it serves. The students' baseline performance must always be your starting point from which you assess the 'gap' between what they actually achieve and what they could achieve.

> **Leaders must know and be able to articulate the context of their school in order to have a baseline to measure progress over time**

For many schools, defining and articulating their **unique context** is their first problem. As a result, they struggle to accurately define students' starting points so that progress can be measured and tracked over time.

Schools are in a constant state of flux and change - students change, teachers change, leaders change, curriculum changes, resources change, parents change, communities change, governors change, school environments change, and regulations change. These ongoing changes in people, resources and direction can undermine signs of progress and school improvement if the school is unclear of it's original starting point. The starting point for self-evaluation is critical; if this is not established effectively then everything that follows is built on an insecure foundation.

Different stakeholders will look at the school from different perspectives, so it is important to engage them in discussion to get a rounded accurate view of the school's context that represents all interests. The following questions should help to stimulate discussion with different stakeholders about the school's starting points.

What assessment tools does your school use to measure students' starting points?

How do you define your school's baseline?

How does your school track and measure students' progress from starting points over time?

How do you define expectations in terms of students' progress?

How often do you review students' progress from starting points?

How is this analysis shared with key stakeholders?

Students – Teachers – Leaders – Parents – Governors

Focal points

Exit examinations and standardised testing are now the norm in most schools. For many schools, accreditation processes, international benchmarks and national education agendas create additional transparent accountability measures and are typically used to evaluate the impact of educational provision on student learning. However, this evaluation of results often ends up looking more like an 'autopsy' of what worked and what didn't rather than a tool to support ongoing self-evaluation of student learning.

> **Reliance on external assessments will simply develop a culture of blame and excuse making**

The problems occur when schools start being driven by a narrow focus on annual results rather than ongoing incremental improvement. Annual markers, used to measure student attainment, are clearly important to measure progress of student cohorts over time, but schools often miss the opportunity to track and make in-house adjustments which is the fundamental purpose of self-evaluation. The key difference is whether the school is **leading** its own improvement, by recognising variations between cohorts of students, through systematic purposeful self-evaluation, or is **lagging** by using self-evaluation to explain different student outcomes and attempt to demonstrate improvement as a response to an external stimulus.

The following questions should help to stimulate discussion with different stakeholders about the school's focal points.

What external tools does your school use to measure student attainment?

How do these measures align with in-house assessment tools?

How often is internal analysis carried out?

How often is external analysis carried out?

How is progress on student outcomes reported, and to whom?

Who is held to account for the impact of this student outcome data analysis?

Pin points

The quality of teaching and learning is directly linked to the quality of student outcomes. A student's progress over time is a direct result of daily improvements made over the course of an academic year or phase of study. Therefore, the quality of learning in your school must be at the heart of your school's strategy for self-evaluation.

Unfortunately, even today, too many schools implement complex programmes of lesson observations and scrutiny of students' work where the focus is too heavily skewed to the quality of teaching taking place rather than the quality of students' learning (as an outcome of the teaching they have received).

What are the characteristics of the school's arrangements that are promoting effective learning for all students?

Ratings of lesson observations which are teacher centred instead of student centred negate the real purpose ... self-evaluation should focus on how well students are learning rather than what teachers are doing.

Schools that are driven by a narrow focus on the quality of teaching are actively encouraging a culture of fear and non-reflective practice on what matters most - student learning and progress within lessons. In this scenario, leaders and teachers focus too much on what they are doing and not on what the students are doing.

The following questions should help to stimulate discussion with different stakeholders about the school's pin points.

What tools do you use to observe and evaluate lessons?

How do you use observations to analyse the quality of learning?

How often is this analysis carried out, and by whom?

How does this analysis impact on improvements in student learning?

Who is held to account for the impact of this lesson observation data analysis?

NOTES

Pressure points

It is really quite simple … the quality of leadership and management is ultimately measured by the quality of learning and the subsequent impact on student outcomes.

In today's busy climate, principals need more than ever to filter inputs from a variety of competing sources and to be constantly challenged to maintain their focus on the most critical priority of student learning.

Distractions come from many directions. They can be disguised as innovation and are usually strong-armed by the loudest, most influential voice at any given time. As a result, a culture of being reactive can prevail if the principal doesn't manage them confidently and effectively. Principals often find themselves playing games of tug-of-war with parents, teachers, governors, regulators, community members and social media - to name a few - whilst trying to maintain a focus on student learning. The day-to-day administrative distractions can also place competing demands on principals if they don't have a strong and purposeful **strategy for self-evaluation** that clearly defines who is responsible and accountable for students' outcomes, performance and results.

> The school's strategy for self-evaluation should focus focus focus on student learning

The following questions should help to stimulate discussion with different stakeholders about the school's pressure points.

What is distracting you (and your school) from focusing on self-evaluation?

How well do all your stakeholders understand their role in self-evaluation and how they impact the quality of education in your school?

How do you ensure all stakeholders know their respective roles, responsibilities and accountabilities with regard to self-evaluation?

How often do you assess the impact of your stakeholders' contribution and performance?

Who is held to account for the impact of stakeholders on your school's self-evaluation?

NOTES
33

The right setting for self-evaluation

There is no magic formula to creating an environment in which self-evaluation can flourish, but there are some underlying principles that will help you to gain some personal clarity, establish a conducive setting and keep the school moving in the right direction at the right speed. It is essential to remember that people carry out self-evaluation and this is where you must initially focus your attention if you want the process to work. Without the people aspect, you will simply have a production line that runs at a pre-set speed and churns out the same thing time after time - this is when self-evaluation becomes a meaningless activity and is essentially a burden on any school.

- Create an inspiring vision for the school
- Create the right environment for people to buy in
- Engage all stakeholders with authenticity and purpose
- Have courage and take responsibility for getting things done
- Create unity and motivate your team to perform
- See obstacles as challenges and opportunities to grow

Create an inspiring vision for the school

Strategy is about big picture and about taking a long-term view that transcends day-to-day operational issues. It is very easy to get sucked into the detail and bogged down in the minutia of daily life in the school, but you must make sure that you filter what is most important and relevant. You can only do this if you have a clear vision of what you are trying to achieve and a representation of what your strategy will actually deliver.

> Establishing a vision takes time but it is time well spent.

> Imagine what the school's future will be like.

> The vision should be clear and simple.

Your vision should be an aspirational description of what the school will look like in the future. It should allow people to see a picture in their mind and imagine what the school will achieve and accomplish, as well as providing them with a clear direction to plan their future goals and actions. If you represent the vision purely in words, then it is critical to be precise in the vocabulary you choose otherwise different stakeholders may have a different interpretation.

As principal, you may understand and appreciate the importance of having a clearly articulated vision, but what about your senior leaders … your middle leaders … your teachers … your governors? Think about bringing these and all other stakeholders together for a session during which you collectively create a vision board that summarises and represents your school's vision, which will then underpin and scaffold the school's self-evaluation.

What makes your school unique and different from the school down the road? Your vision needs to answer this question and should serve as a marketing tool to convince potential parents that this is the school community that their children need to be part of. Producing a vision and engaging in self-evaluation and improvement are not unique to schools, so reading about approaches outside education can help you think in a different way and see things from a different perspective – look to other cultures, education systems and the world of business for inspiration.

> Reflection on the vision and its support for self-evaluation in your school

Create the right environment for people to buy in

This may sound a little obvious, but you might be surprised by the number of times school leaders struggle with some of the things they are asked to do in the name of self-evaluation. One of the biggest barriers to successful self-evaluation is when people blindly take part in activities where they have little emotional investment. In other words, they are simply going through the motions. Although this may ensure that the processes run and that some form of evaluation activity actually takes place, it is neither a useful nor profitable approach and wastes precious time and energy. Realistically, every day, we all have to do some things we would rather not do. What is effective is when each individual realises the value they bring to the self-evaluation process which, initially, may seem irrelevant and unrelated to their perceived specific responsibilities.

> So how do you create the right environment for people to buy in to self-evaluation?
>
> Basically, you have to live your values and lead by example.
>
> As principal, the buck may stop with you, but you cannot do it alone!

Demonstrate integrity by following your own advice, being honest and treating others the way you wish to be treated. In the context of self-evaluation, this means challenging yourself about what you are asking other people to do and being sure that your motives are clear enough and they understand why this action is important. By focusing on the **why** rather than the **what** or **how**, you will increase buy-in and subsequently accelerate the pace and speed of the process.

Practice humility by not letting your ego control your thoughts and actions. Instead of comparing yourself and your school to others – and then trying to do everything yourself – focus on how you can help the people around you to achieve their part of the evaluation and improvement process.

Share your gratitude. Schools can only realise their strategy by working in teams and it is important to build in opportunities for recognition and acknowledgment of this. The most effective schools distribute their self-evaluation across all parts of their community.

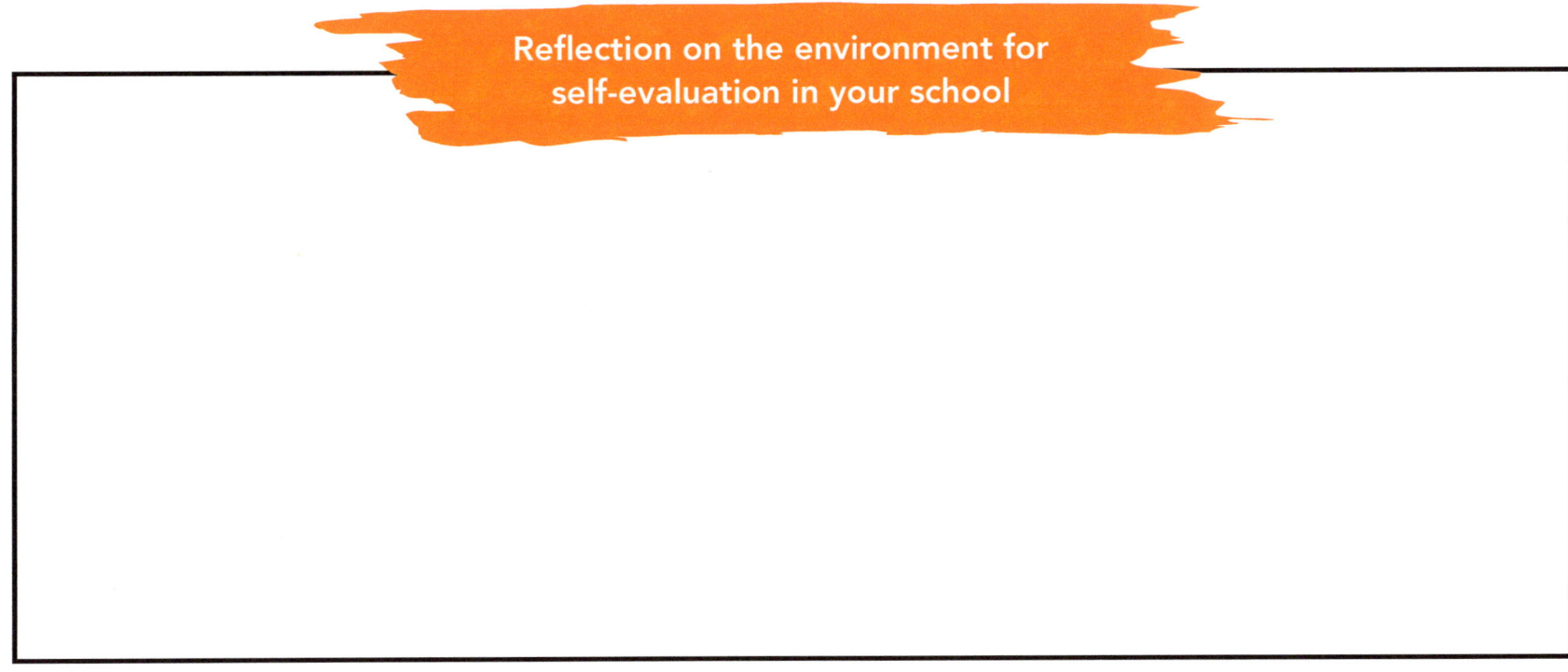

Reflection on the environment for self-evaluation in your school

Engage all stakeholders with authenticity and purpose

The most important thing to remember is that everyone must be pulling in the same direction and share a sense of urgency to make things happen. As principal, you need to be explicit about everyone's responsibilities and set clear expectations and boundaries. Each individual should be able to explain their key priority – the main focus in their area of responsibility at any given point in time – and then be able to articulate how this contributes to both evaluation and improvement in the school.

Reflection on how you engage stakeholders in self-evaluation in your school

Have courage and take responsibility for getting things done

It is important to realise that, although exterior conditions do have an impact, it is your internal decisions that are far more important when it comes to the actions you take and the type of school you are striving to create. As principal, your job is simply to take charge of the school's self-evaluation, which requires responsibility, courage and discipline. Now that you have ensured that everyone understands the contribution they are expected to make to self-evaluation, your job is to set key targets and milestones that will allow you, and your senior leaders, to take the pulse and manage the rhythm of school improvement.

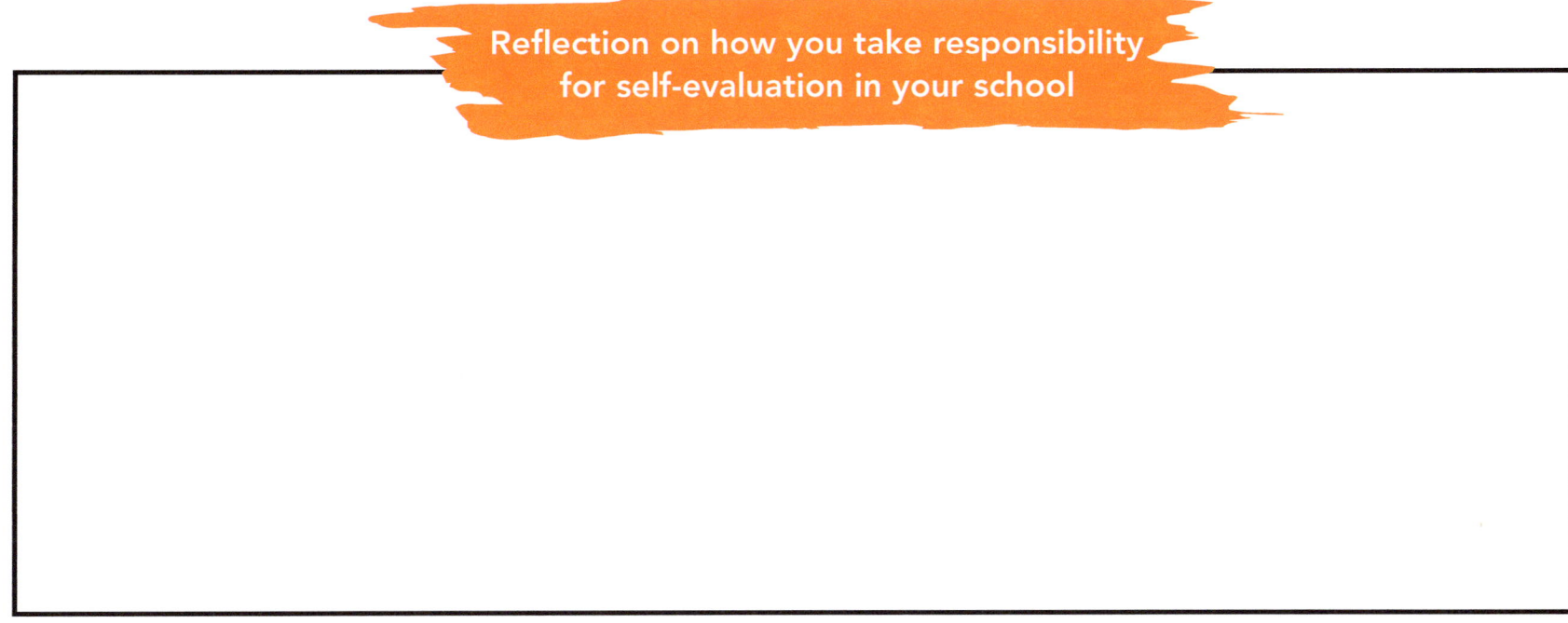

Reflection on how you take responsibility for self-evaluation in your school

Create unity and motivate your team to perform

The successful delivery of your school's self-evaluation will depend and rely on the people who implement the process. It is very rare that schools do not have some appropriate processes in place, but it is much more likely that they do not have consistent behaviours among their people. As principal, you need to understand how to motivate the different individuals on your teams and ensure that everyone understands that successful teams deliver more than the sum of each individual's effort. There will inevitably be times when it would be quicker for you to do things yourself but demonstrating respect and empathy in the workplace means showing others that their ideas and opinions are valued. If someone makes a suggestion it is important that their voice is heard and that you, and their colleagues, do not dismiss it too quickly. Team building is a learned skill and fundamental to that skill is the ability to identify the individual's voice and ensure that voice is recognised by the wider group.

Reflection on how you motivate teams for self-evaluation in your school

See obstacles as challenges and opportunities to grow

Having a **strategy** for school-led self-evaluation is important but having the capacity to be flexible and adaptable when circumstances change is just as important. There are inevitably times when the unexpected will occur and you are faced with giving up or pushing through – this is where resilience and perseverance come into play.

The speed at which your school will deliver its self-evaluation is as much about managing the challenges and obstacles that get in your way than aligning performance with targets and goals. If you have someone on your team that you know is skilled in an area you may be lacking, don't be afraid to go and ask them for help – remember everyone has a special talent and skill looking for an opportunity to shine and add value.

Despite their hierarchical position in the school, principals are often left feeling vulnerable and isolated, especially when things are not going well. As principal, you need to accept that feedback is rarely intended to insult – even when it may appear blunt and negative. It is important to learn to take whatever truth there may be in the criticism and act to move forward rather than dwell on it.

> Never give up!
>
> We often underestimate the time and amount of effort a goal will take to achieve.
>
> Instead of giving up or lowering the mark, give yourself more time and/or increase your efforts.

Schools are learning organisations and, as such, have developed highly effective systems for reflection, review and development that are applied to personalise students' learning. It should therefore be a relatively easy and natural progression to extend this same philosophy to a school's self-evaluation to ensure that it is truly personalised to the needs of the school.

Reflect – what is working well and what is not?

Review – what challenges and obstacles are we facing?

Develop – what can we do differently to make sure our self-evaluation remains fit for purpose?

Reflection on how you address self-evaluation challenges and opportunities in your school

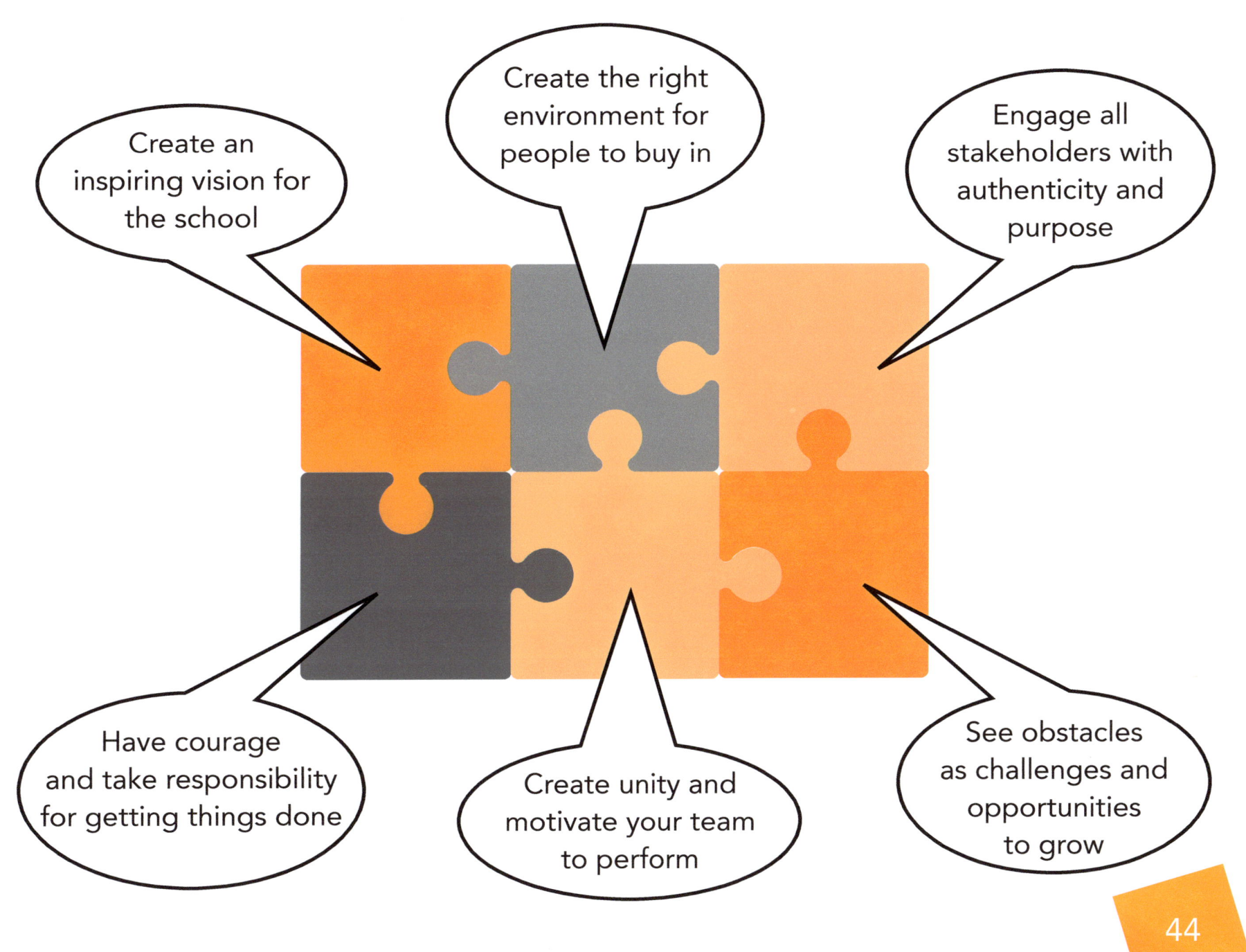

Levels of self-evaluation

Self-evaluation takes place at a number of levels in a school and it is essential that the different outcomes from each level are recognised and considered as part of the school's high level strategic planning. If this doesn't happen then self-evaluation simply becomes a process that is carried out without a clear purpose. It becomes a 'bolt on' series of activities that often starts to take over from other important activities and functions in the school.

Micro

The focus is on the detail of what is happening in the individual classrooms.

This level is typically characterised by a high volume of lesson observations, work scrutiny and student voice activities.

Macro

The focus is on the whole school taking the priorities in the school improvement plan as the big picture to drive self-evaluation.

This level usually concentrates on analysis of data from assessments and external examinations but can also involve input from other stakeholders, such as parental and local community evaluations.

Means end

The focus is on how well the school's evaluation drives leadership decisions that strengthens its improvement planning to have an impact on the quality of students' learning.

This level gives self-evaluation a clear purpose from a leadership perspective and should be fully integrated into the school.

Means end self-evaluation

Self-evaluation is no use whatsoever unless it is embedded into the school's planning and improvement cycle. As a process, it should be so well integrated into the daily life of the school that it helps to monitor the impact of decisions that have been taken, and the subsequent actions that have been implemented, at regular intervals. If self-evaluation is seen as a separate or tangential activity to the rest of the school's functions, then it will flounder and the school's vital signs will begin to fail.

> **Your school's self-evaluation should be driven internally and should not be a reaction to external factors and influences**

A **means to an end** is something that is done only to produce a desired result and is therefore any action (the means) carried out for the purpose of achieving something else (an end). Taking this definition … when self-evaluation is the **means**, it must have a clear purpose and be done to produce a desired result. In this case, the **end** is an evaluation of how well the school's leadership decisions have driven its improvement planning and given rise to a positive impact on students' learning and educational outcomes. Means end self-evaluation therefore requires collaborative effort and joined up thinking – a clear **strategy** will help to define this.

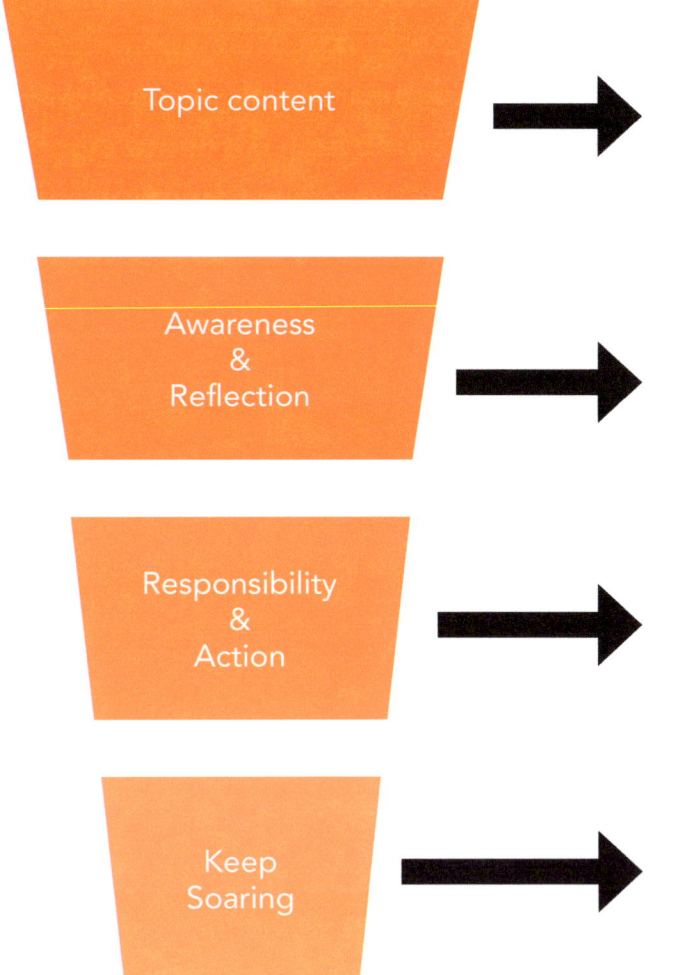

Topic content

Awareness & Reflection

Responsibility & Action

Keep Soaring

In this chapter, we have focused on the need to have a clear **purpose** for the school's self-evaluation to ensure that all the **people** are involved in an authentic and meaningful **process**. We have identified the need to create the vision, environment and collaboration to integrate and embed self-evaluation so that it fulfils the purpose of evaluating the school's leadership decisions on planning for improvement and the subsequent impact on the learning and outcomes for students.

The key questions on the following pages should help you to reflect and articulate the current situation, with regard to the **purpose** of self-evaluation in your school.

Taking the main messages from this chapter, and the outcomes from your reflection, use the NOTES page to identify what needs to happen next and how this will be implemented to strengthen the **purpose** of your school's self-evaluation.

Select **one leadership decision** that has been taken and now needs to form the basis of subsequent self-evaluation activity in your school. Complete the highlighted sections on the Keep Soaring flight plan on page 54.

47

PURPOSE: KEY INSIGHTS

Which levels of self-evaluation are currently operating in your school?

To what extent are different groups of students learning and achieving?

Which groups of students does your school improvement currently focus on (and why)?

To what extent is your school improvement planning having an impact on the learning and outcomes for these groups of students?

How do you know there is an end (improvement) to your means (self-evaluation)?

What are the key leadership decisions that have been made and need to be used to define your school's current self-evaluation purpose?

NOTES

FLIGHT PLAN

PURPOSE

The leadership decision that has been taken that will form the focus of your self-evaluation

MEANS

Where are the actions arising from this decision planned?

END

What metrics will be used to show improved performance as a result of this decision?

IMPACT

Where do you expect to measure the impact?

Which groups of students will show improved performance?

What will you measure?

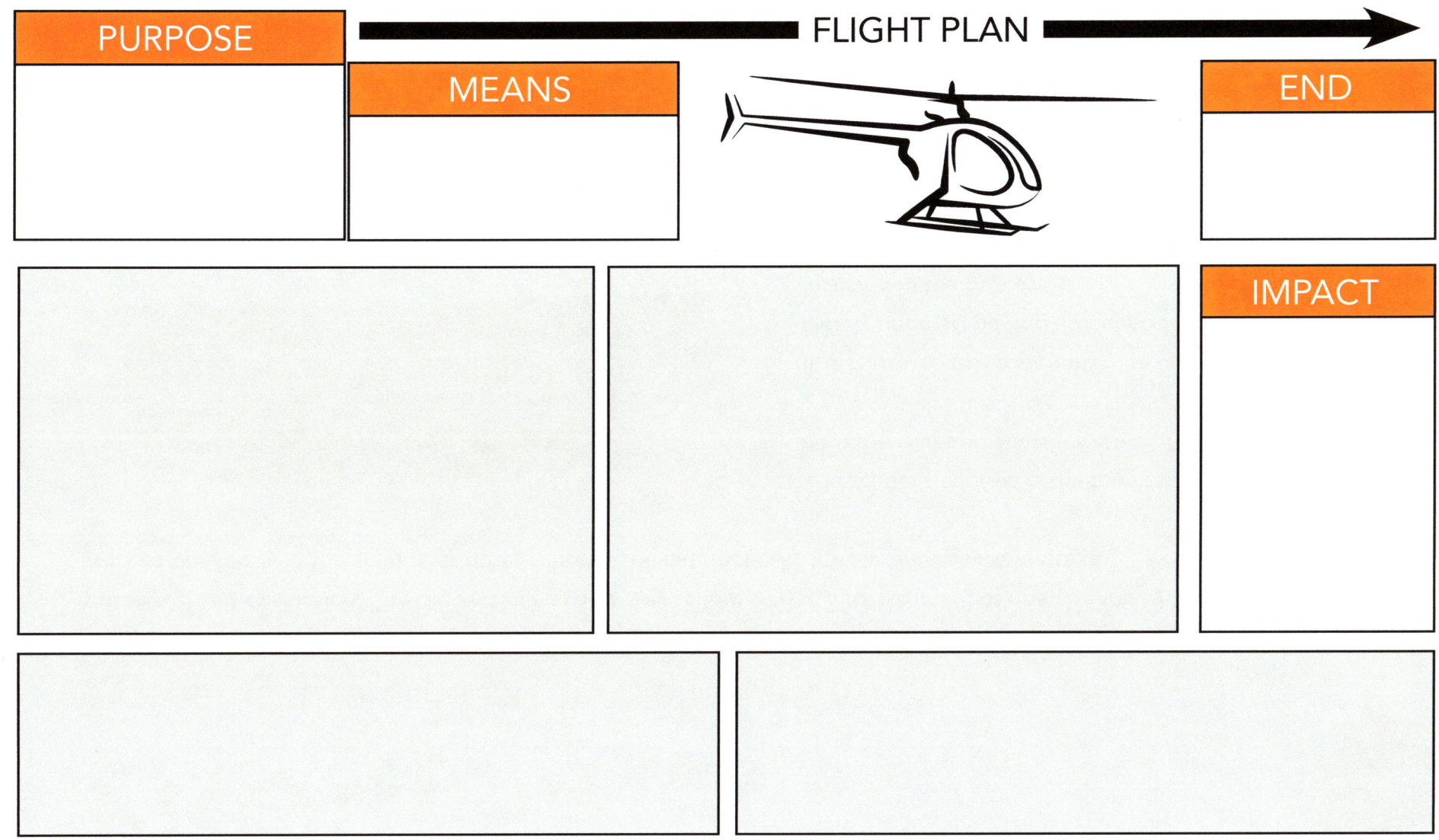

PROCESS

Agreeing the context for self-evaluation

Every school is different and is a dynamic community that brings its own unique strengths and challenges to the process of self-evaluation. The biggest mistake for any school leader is to assume that one size fits all and that what has worked previously in the school, or other schools, will automatically transfer into a new context.

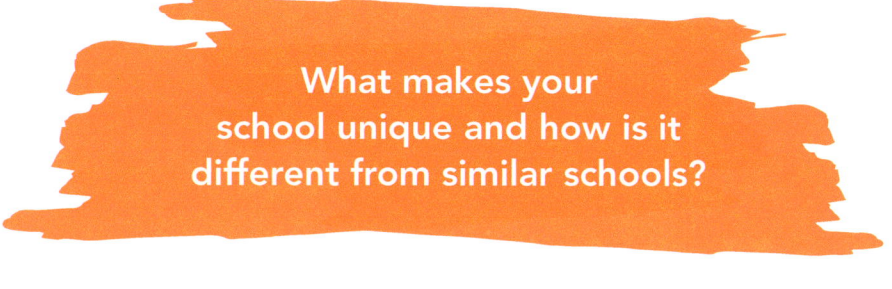

What makes your school unique and how is it different from similar schools?

The school's context is the foundation on which all self-evaluation activities are built.

It is critical to make sure that the context is clearly understood and articulated to everyone involved in the process.

Taking time to get this right at the start will provide a secure platform for all future activity but unfortunately too many schools skip this and make assumptions that everyone views the school in the same way. Each stakeholder group will look at the school from their own perspective. This is why it is so important to clarify and define the context to establish a consistent foundation for all self-evaluation activity.

How would you describe your school's geographical location and cultural context?

What local/national factors influence the school?

How would you describe your school's governance structure?

What do your governors expect from the school?

How would you describe your school's parental population?

What do your parents expect from the school?

How would you describe your school's staffing situation?

Class teachers	Middle leaders	Senior leaders	Other classroom staff	Administrative staff

Considering the make-up of each different cohort of students, how would you describe your school's student population?

Age 3	Age 4-5	Age 5-6	Age 6-7	Age 7-8
Age 8-9	Age 9-10	Age 10-11	Age 11-12	Age 12-13
Age 13-14	Age 14-15	Age 15-16	Age 16-17	Age 17-18

Schools are living dynamic organisations that can change very quickly and it is important to remember that one small change, whether in staffing or the composition of an individual class of students, can have a significant ripple effect throughout the whole school. This is why it is so important that your school has a process by which their contextual information is regularly checked, reviewed and updated.

> **?** How accurate and appropriately evidenced are your senior and middle leaders' views of each cohort of students?

Schools generate and hold so much data on students that the issue is often one of information overload rather than omission.

> **If you were to collect ALL the data held on an individual student in your school – where would you get it from and what would it look like?**

Heads of Year typically maintain an overview of the students in their respective year group, but this information is often more pastoral in nature and is a diluted version that provides an incomplete snapshot of individual student academic performance.

Secondary form tutors typically maintain information for individual groups of students – they are likely to record personal information and attendance data for each student.

Early years, primary class teachers and subject teachers typically maintain information for their individual classes – they record student information and assessment data relevant to their lessons and individual student's learning.

Specialist support staff typically maintain information for the students they work with – they record the outcomes of any intervention activities and data on students' learning and progress towards agreed targets.

School leaders are accountable for understanding, monitoring and evaluating the learning of the 'whole child' in the school context, therefore it is essential to have the relevant data readily available on all students within a cohort. So how do you make this meaningful yet manageable? A useful approach is to create a single page dashboard for each cohort of students by drawing together the most relevant data from all the individual sources within the school. Although this may sound like repetition, it is an increasingly important activity that provides a sense check at a number of levels and ensures that anyone can see, at a glance, the contextual factors that are prevalent in that group of students.

What are the contextual factors relevant to this cohort of students?

Are you collecting the right data at the right time(s) for these students?

How do you explain the performance of this cohort in relation to their context within the school?

What interventions are required to counter-balance the contextual factors that are influencing this group of students?

Methodology of self-evaluation

Many countries around the world have developed and introduced national inspection systems with the key intention of providing quality management systems to drive improvement in school standards. Increasingly, robust and authentic self-evaluation at individual school level is becoming one of the defining measures for both leadership and overall school performance judgements. It doesn't matter which education system you are delivering, or which Government authority is regulating and inspecting your school, the core methodology of self-evaluation remains the same.

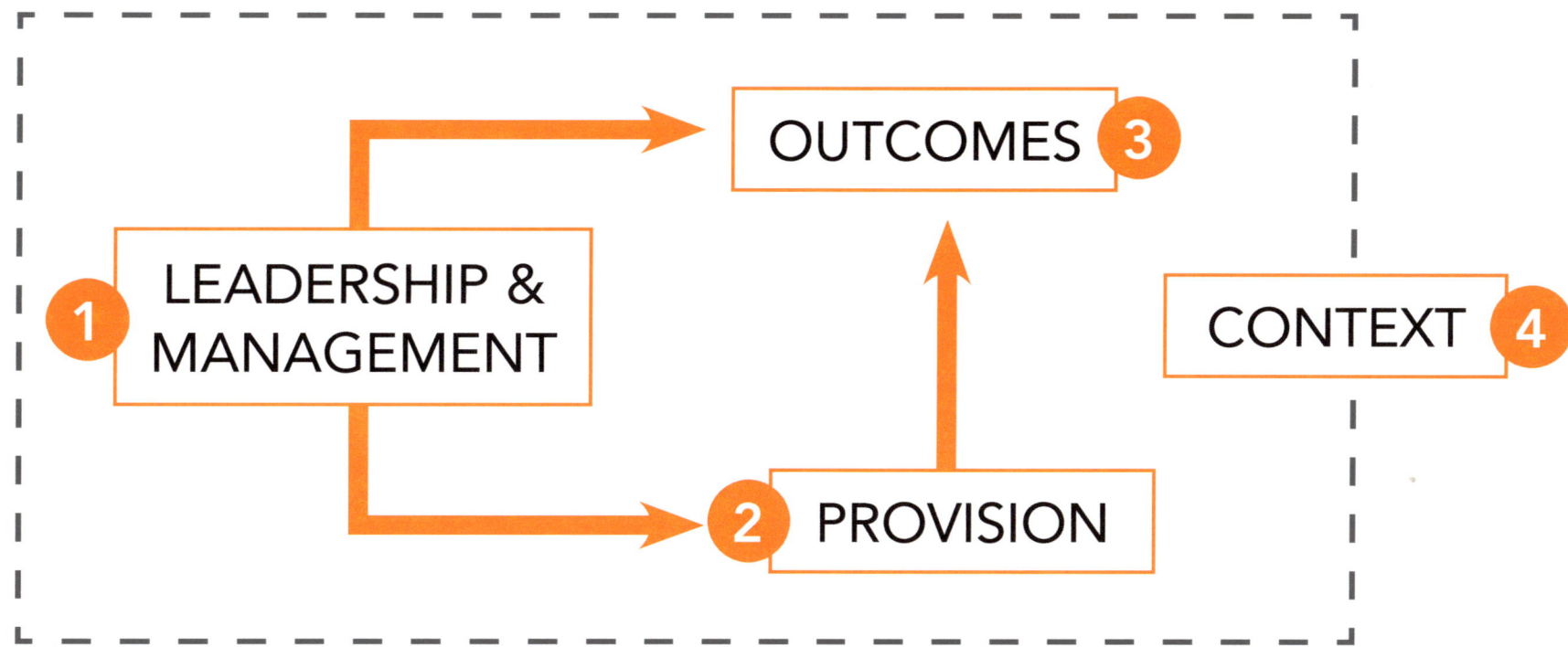

The first mistake that many schools make is to focus their initial attention purely on the outcomes, i.e. examination results and students' academic performance. This is understandable since schools are increasingly judged by comparison against other schools in league tables and other ranked systems. However, please notice that outcomes is number (3) on the diagram while leadership & management is number (1).

Why is this a mistake?

Because the outcomes in any school must be judged in the context of that particular school and against the backdrop of the leadership and management decisions that have been taken as a result.

In other words …

Inspection, and other external quality assurance processes, quite rightly place an emphasis on student outcomes as a comparative measure across different schools. However, self-evaluation is an internal process within a school and **means end self-evaluation** should be determining the impact of the school's decision making and improvement planning on its overall effectiveness.

Self-evaluation is not a replica for inspection - are you implementing self-evaluation or self-inspection?

Self-evaluation should always start with the key decisions that have been taken by the school's leadership set in the context of their individual school.

63

1 # LEADERSHIP & MANAGEMENT
What are the key decisions that your school has taken?
Why were these the decisions that have been implemented (evidence based)?

2 # PROVISION
How have these decisions impacted what the school provides for students?
Curriculum, Interventions, Support Activities, Enhancements, Quality of Teaching …

3 # OUTCOMES
What evidence is there that these changes in the school's provision have impacted on student outcomes (academic and personal development)?

4 # CONTEXT
Considering this evidence, and in the context of **these students**, what has to happen next? What *leadership and management* decisions **now** have to be taken in light of the evidence of impact on students?

IMPACT

So what?

Yes – it is true – inspectors are often taught and encouraged to ask this question! But this is one of the most powerful questions you can learn to use in your own school. Often, teachers and senior leaders get too wrapped up in data and think that the more they produce (quantity) and the prettier they make it look by producing ever increasingly complex charts and tables (a skewed perception of quality) the better it is and the more it tells them.

Try this simple exercise:

Select a subject leader at random and ask them to show you how they (as a leader of a subject in your school) record the most important data on student outcomes and use it to make evidence-based decisions.

> How many spreadsheets do they show you?
> How many tables of raw data do you see?
> How many colour coded bar charts, pie charts and other graphs have they produced?

Now ask yourself ... so what?

You already know the teacher is capable of using a spreadsheet, producing tables and drawing graphs but what does all of this data tell you instantly about the performance of the students in that subject and the priority decisions that subject leader is making based on this evidence?

One of the reasons some teachers and middle leaders are often resistant to self-evaluation is that they believe it increases workload by creating another layer of bureaucracy and paperwork. These are the schools where there is always a last minute scramble to collect and present the data and evidence required when they are notified of an impending external evaluation, such as inspection, audit or accreditation visit.

65

If you are genuinely implementing a meaningful and **authentic self-evaluation** process, then you will be collecting, recording, analysing and using data to drive your ongoing school decision-making. By starting with the leadership and management focus, you will have a much clearer understanding of the data you need and can therefore manage the entire process to prevent overload and prevent the broad-brush approach that many schools take purely by default.

If everyone involved in self-evaluation genuinely understands the context of your school and the student cohort profiles …

AND

All leadership decisions are driven by quality assured evidence collected through self-evaluation in relation to the school's context at that time …

THEN

Self-evaluation engages everyone in a meaningful and useful process to monitor, measure and celebrate the school's improvement

Evaluation trails

One of the biggest challenges for a principal is to accept that you can't do everything all at once. There will be times in every school's evolution that the 'To Do' list becomes overwhelming and this is when it is crucial to be able to step back, take an objective view and identify the most appropriate priority for development.

The standard definition of priority is that it is the one thing that is considered of greater importance than all others at any given point in time. By trying to tackle multiple priorities at the same time, are you really having the impact you could if you focused on one single priority for a designated period of time and gave it everything you had?

Obviously, across the school you will have a number of key stakeholders involved in the self-evaluation process. Typically, they will all set multiple priorities aligned with the school's overall improvement plan, but how do you ensure that each of them is working on the issue of greatest importance to their area of responsibility, i.e. the one that will have the greatest impact on students and their outcomes?

Senior and middle leaders usually use the school's annual improvement plan to guide their own planning, whether by subject, year group or aspect of the school's work. One way to help these leaders get their priorities into focus is to set the background agenda more precisely by identifying a number of **evaluation trails** that arise from the school's improvement plan. An evaluation trail should follow the methodology flow shown on page 62.

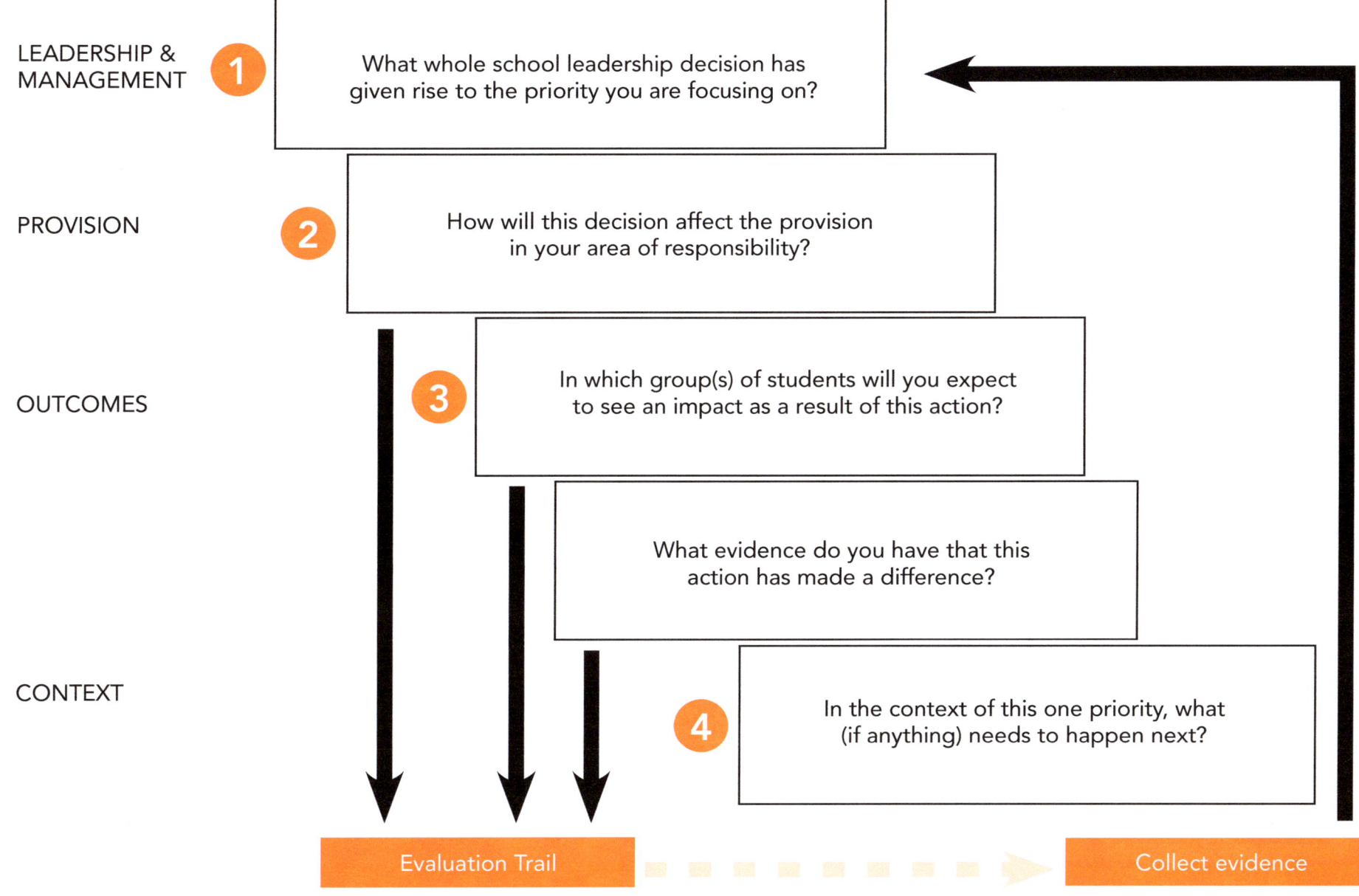

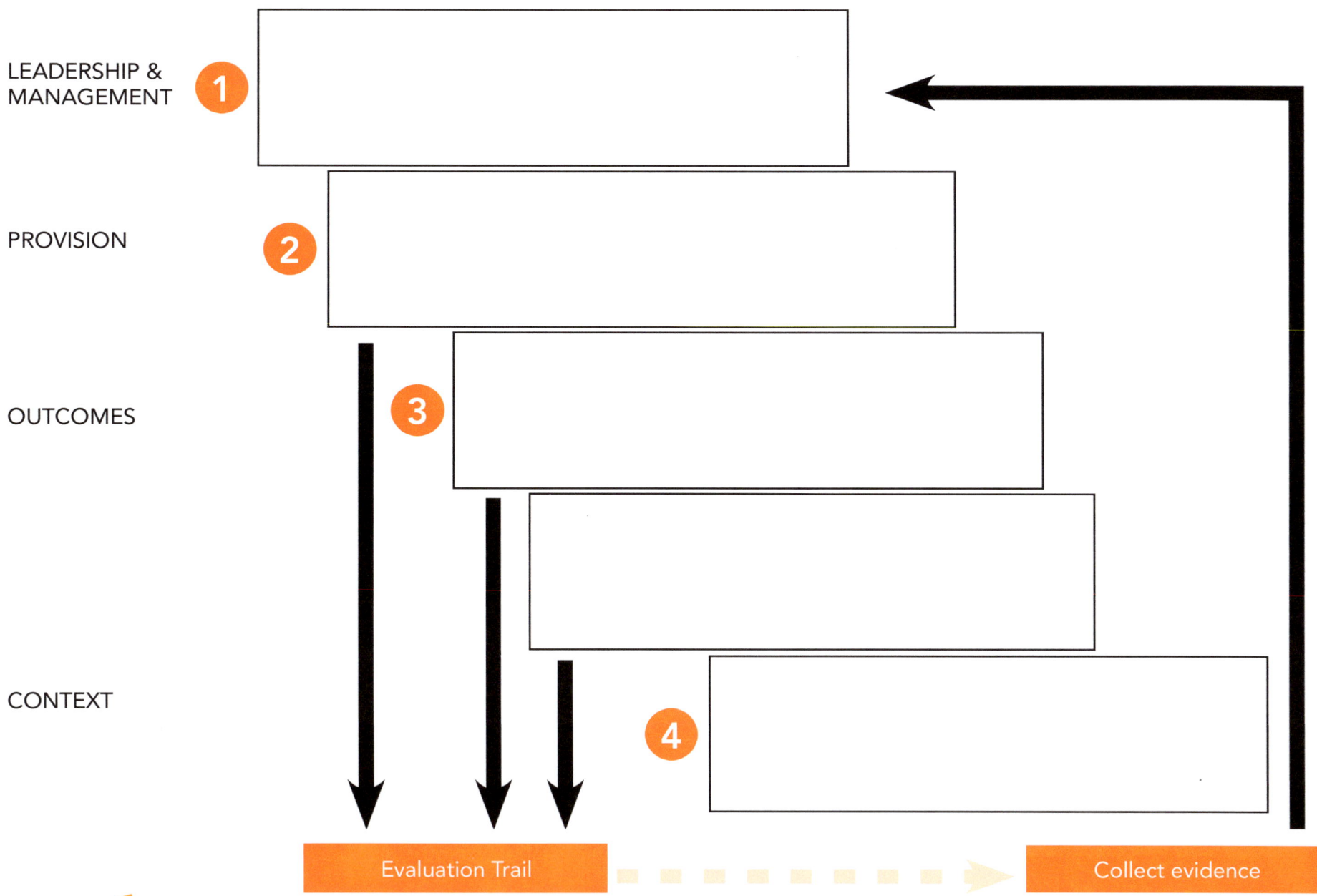

LEADERSHIP &
MANAGEMENT **1**

PROVISION **2**

OUTCOMES **3**

CONTEXT **4**

Evaluation Trail   Collect evidence

The following questions should help to stimulate discussion with different stakeholders about the school's context and the most relevant evaluation trails arising from this context.

What makes your school unique?

How do you define the context for your school?

How do you capture and define the context for different cohorts of students?

What are the key leadership decisions that have been taken that are currently driving your school's focus on improvement?

How do you focus and plan the activities in your current self-evaluation process?

How do you align this approach to evaluation trails with the purpose of evaluating the impact of your leadership decisions?

Collecting evidence through self-evaluation

Leadership and management decisions need to be based on quality assured evidence of student learning and staff performance. If evidence collected is not linked to purpose then staff will complain about workload and subsequently, they will not link this evidence to their decision making, planning and action. The analysis of this evidence must be accurate and lead to further leadership decisions and actions to demonstrate ongoing, continuous school improvement. There are many aspects to a successful self-evaluation process but it will ultimately stand or fall upon the skills of your people to accurately interpret the evidence and take subsequent action.

What kind of evidence do we need?

There are three sources of evidence that need to be represented in all self-evaluation activities.

Observation is where you see something happen first-hand and record some evidence at that point in time.

Discussion is where evidence is collected through verbal communication with another individual (student, colleague, parent, etc.)

Documentation is where something is recorded by being written down (policies, assessment records, etc.)

How much evidence is enough?

The quality of evidence is so much more important than the quantity of evidence collected, so how do you know when you have got enough? The most reliable way is to implement a process of **triangulation** in collecting self-evaluation evidence. The rules for triangulation are simple and can be easily translated into any self-evaluation activity – collect sufficient evidence from all three sources and, assuming they agree and validate each other, then you should be confident that your judgements and subsequent evaluation are robust and reliable.

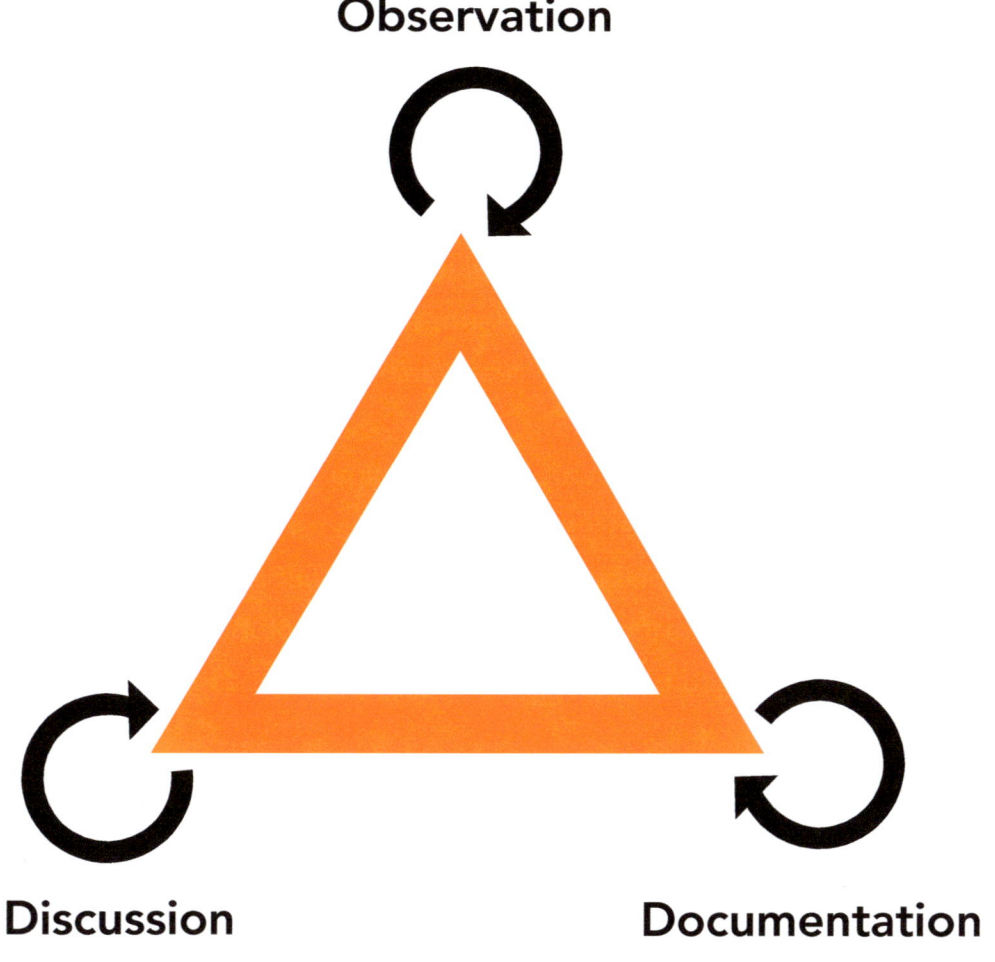

Aim to collect sufficient evidence from EACH of the three sources to triangulate your judgement

Observation is the most reliable source of evidence – actually seeing something happen with your own eyes

Discussion is the next reliable source of evidence – talking to someone and getting their evaluation and perspective

Documentation is the least reliable source of evidence – just because something is written down doesn't mean it happens effectively

Scheduling self-evaluation

A robust self-evaluation schedule is the very foundation upon which your self-evaluation is built. It depends on the inter-relationship and co-dependency of several internal and external factors, such as how the school organises the timetable, assigns students and teachers to classes, and develops the calendar of events for regulatory or governance activities, including inspection or accreditation and standardised tests and examinations.

Internal factors

Over decades, schools have developed a natural pulse and rhythm to the academic year. Students are traditionally placed in grades based on their birthdate and usually move from grade to grade on an annual basis. Students are typically assigned to classes, teachers and courses depending on their grade/age and sometimes based on their ability. Teachers are usually assigned to classes and grades based on their experience and qualifications. Teachers can have several classes within a subject area or teach several subjects to one class depending on how the school organises itself.

Most schools have a very clear vision and set of processes for designing their timetable based on agreed principles related to staff working time, instructional hours and course curriculum requirements. The school timetable also impacts the scheduling of staff meeting times, collaborative planning times, performance reviews and appraisals of staff responsible for student outcomes. Additionally, schools develop their calendars of events based on agreed school and public holidays creating natural breaks, terms or semesters of learning, assessment and reporting of student outcomes.

External factors

The scheduling of self-evaluation activities also depends on several external factors which impact a school's timeline for data review and analysis; namely governing body reports, inspection/accreditation events and results, end of year examinations and results, standardised testing events and results.

> The school's calendar of events will provide opportunities for continuous self-evaluation activity

Self-evaluation should never be a bolt-on process in a school but should be carefully scheduled to integrate and embed into routine professional practice. Your **strategy** for self-evaluation must take all these internal and external factors into account to ensure that the process will provide the people with accurate, reliable and valid evidence about the impact of school improvement initiatives at the right time.

What are the most significant and relevant internal and external factors that are likely to influence the self-evaluation process in your school?

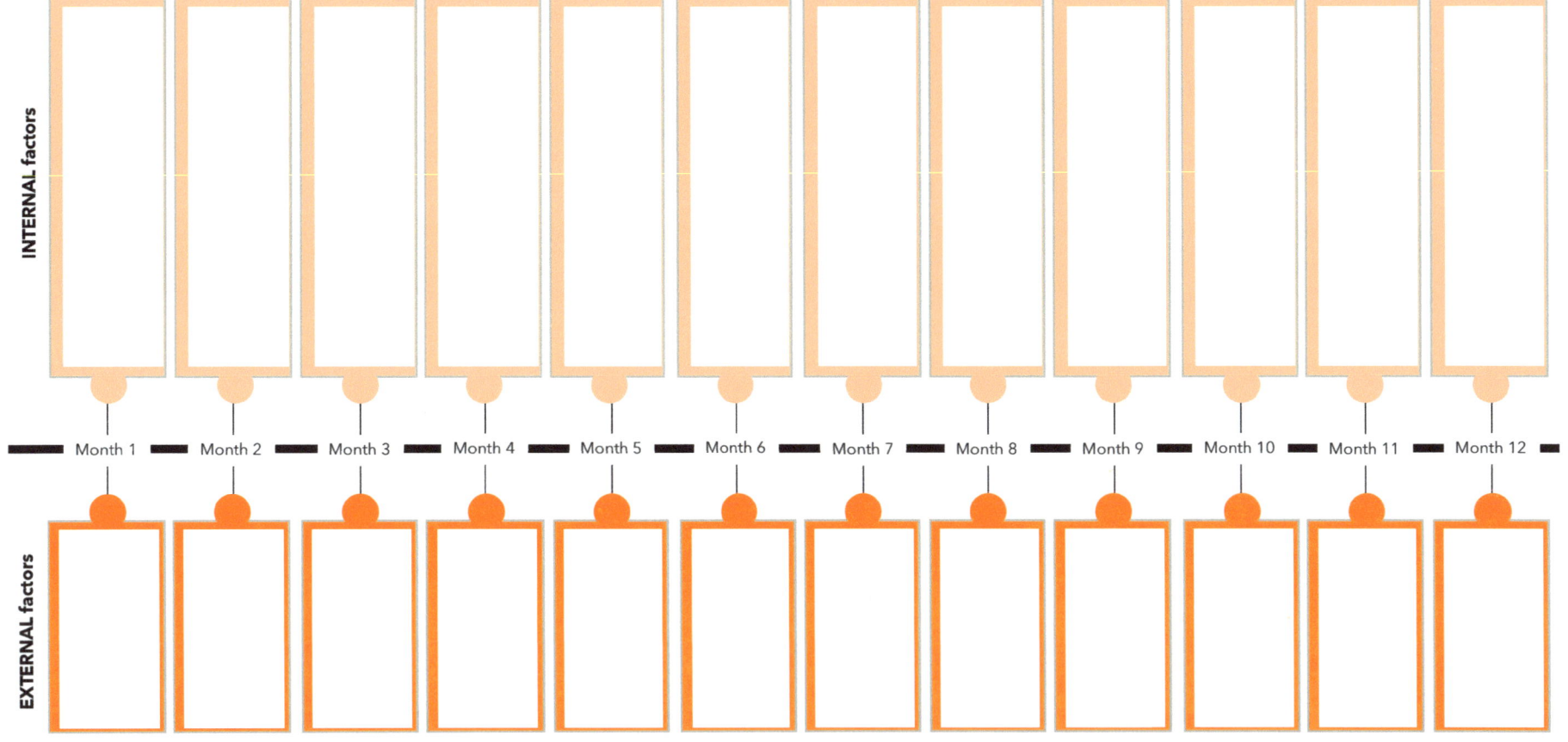

The speed of self-evaluation

We have already established that self-evaluation has a pulse and a rhythm and that the activities that take place need to be scheduled into the day-to-day life of the school. Like any process, there will be variations in speed – an ebb and flow – that will be linked to the attention and demands being placed on the school at different points in its cycle.

Progress towards the desired outcomes is accelerated when all stakeholders:

> share the same values
> are aligned to the processes of self-evaluation
> hold themselves to account through key performance metrics

Therefore, the systems and schedules that the principal and senior leaders put in place to engage and align all stakeholders with the self-evaluation process are fundamental to its success. Principals cannot do everything and delegation of monitoring, measurement and accountability to senior leaders is essential to ensure the avoidance of bottle-necks. Senior leaders need to have the right tools to monitor and measure and thereby allow you to take corrective action when needed.

It is widely accepted that the best way to make any improvement is to focus on the actions needed to create small incremental improvements over time. For instance, to identify that you need to make a 10% improvement in something is quite a daunting realisation, but to consider making 1% improvement – and then replicating this until you have achieved the desired outcome – is not only more manageable but is also much more realistic. If you apply the philosophy of working in manageable chunks to your school's self-evaluation then your choices and actions, taken on a daily basis, can realistically compound to accelerate the school's improvement.

This will only happen if:

> the **right** decisions are taken
> on the basis of the **right** evidence
> for the **right** reasons
> at the **right** time
> leading to the **right** actions being put into place

We have agreed that everyone has a role to play in the school's self-evaluation, but not everyone will be doing the same thing at the same time – they will be working at different speeds to fit into the natural pulse and rhythm of the school. This takes us back to the need for efficient and effective school-led self-evaluation with a clear strategic intent to drive improvement in student outcomes over time … otherwise how do you know what is right for your school?

So how do you achieve this?

As principal, it is your responsibility to engage, inspire and motivate all stakeholders. You need to connect and engage all the different people with the school's core purpose and key priority. Too often, the different stakeholder groups in a school have different priorities and, although each may be comfortable with their individual focus, the cumulative effect can create overload. This is why so many school improvement plans become large unworkable documents that actually do little to drive improvement at grassroots level.

If everybody focused on just **one** thing at the same time … how much progress and improvement could you make in 30 days? This message is clear but is also often very uncomfortable for some schools because it requires a shift in mindset and approach.

Instead of tackling a number of issues at the same time – and thereby diluting the impact of any actions taken – have the courage to step back and work on one key priority that will add meaning and purpose to everyone's action. If everyone has the same core purpose and focuses their efforts for an allocated period of time (e.g. 30 days) this helps avoid distractions and can **accelerate** the **impact** on improvement.

But what about everything else we have to do?

This is the standard objection and reinforces the scattergun approach that too many schools appear quick to accept. If the school has a clear **strategy** for self-evaluation, then you will already be focussing on the things that really matter. The other areas for improvement will be identified and scheduled for attention but, unless they are one of the key leadership decisions being evaluated, they will not be the focus for self-evaluation at this point in time.

At this point, let's consider three other elements of a school that support all aspects of its work – vision, mission and values. Your vision is the big picture of what you are trying to achieve and illustrates where you are going as a school. Your mission is what you are doing to work towards this vision and your values are the beliefs and behaviours that guide this work. It is worth remembering that vision without action is simply an aspiration, while action without vision is simply keeping busy … it is therefore essential to combine vision and action to make things happen.

The speed of self-evaluation is therefore intrinsically linked to effective strategy and planning. Each stakeholder needs to be held to account for their participation and, as principal, you are responsible for creating a culture that values their contribution and focuses their undivided attention on what really matters at that point in time.

Try this exercise ….

1. Summarise your key school beliefs and your high-level goals from your strategic planning document in terms of student performance (outcomes you expect) and staff accountability (quality of teaching and learning).
2. Consider how one individual and/or department in your school will operationalise these goals over the year.
3. Identify how you will measure the impact of these actions on student outcomes.

SCHOOL BELIEFS	REVIEW CYCLE	STRATEGIC GOALS	OPERATIONAL PLANS	IMPACT
VISION Where are you going?	Student Performance			
MISSION What are you doing?				
PURPOSE Why are you doing?	Staff Accountability			
VALUES How are you doing?				

If you have a clear **strategy** for self-evaluation, the **process** and **people** will have a **purpose** and do the right things and **improvement** will happen.

Schools that adopt a long-term strategic overview (vision) supported by a much more focused short-term operational planning approach (action) typically demonstrate improvement in key areas.

Schools that align their self-evaluation (means) to the achievement of their vision (end) typically accelerate improvement in key areas.

Schools that establish a strategy for their self-evaluation, to demonstrate there is an end to their means, typically accelerate improvement in key areas and also improve their effectiveness overall.

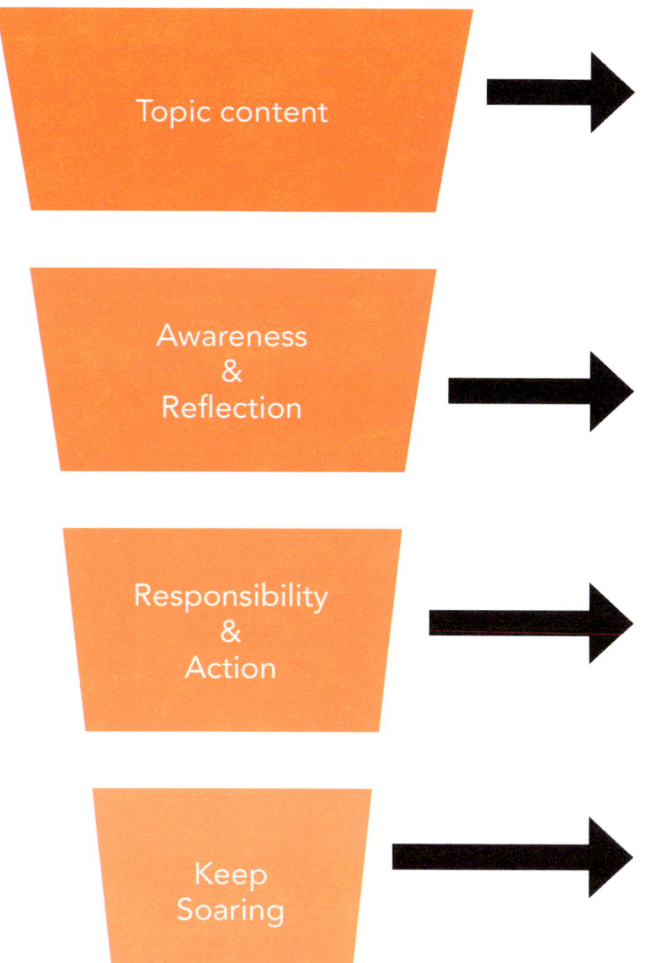

In this chapter, we have focused on the need to have a clearly defined and systematic **process** for the school's self- evaluation to ensure that all the people are involved and are working towards a common purpose. We have reinforced the need to align the school's strategic and operational planning with its vision, and to establish self-evaluation as a process that demonstrates a means to an end (i.e. the impact of the school's leadership decisions and improvement planning on students' outcomes and performance).

The key questions on the following pages should help you to reflect and articulate the current situation, with regard to the **process** of self-evaluation in your school.

Taking the main messages from this chapter, and the outcomes from your reflection, use the NOTES page to identify what needs to happen next with regard to the **process** of your school's self-evaluation.

Using the **same leadership decision** from the previous chapter, complete the highlighted sections on the Keep Soaring flight plan on page 90.

PROCESS: KEY INSIGHTS

How does your self-evaluation process integrate into the school's routine schedule of activities and calendar of events?

How does your self-evaluation process align with the methodology on page 62 to evaluate the school's leadership decisions against the impact of these decisions (and subsequent actions) on students' outcomes?

What are the key evaluation trails arising from the school's current context and leadership decisions?

How does your self-evaluation process ensure that the right evidence is collected for each evaluation trail?

How does your self-evaluation process ensure that evidence collected is triangulated to provide robust quality assured evaluation?

How does your self-evaluation process strengthen the school's improvement planning?

NOTES

FLIGHT PLAN

PROCESS

What self-evaluation activities will be implemented?

How do these activities map into the schedule and calendar of the school?

EVIDENCE

What sources of evidence will be required?

How will evidence be interpreted, triangulated and evaluated?

How will evidence be quality assured?

REVIEW

What checkpoints will be used to review and monitor the effectiveness of the school's self-evaluation of this leadership decision?

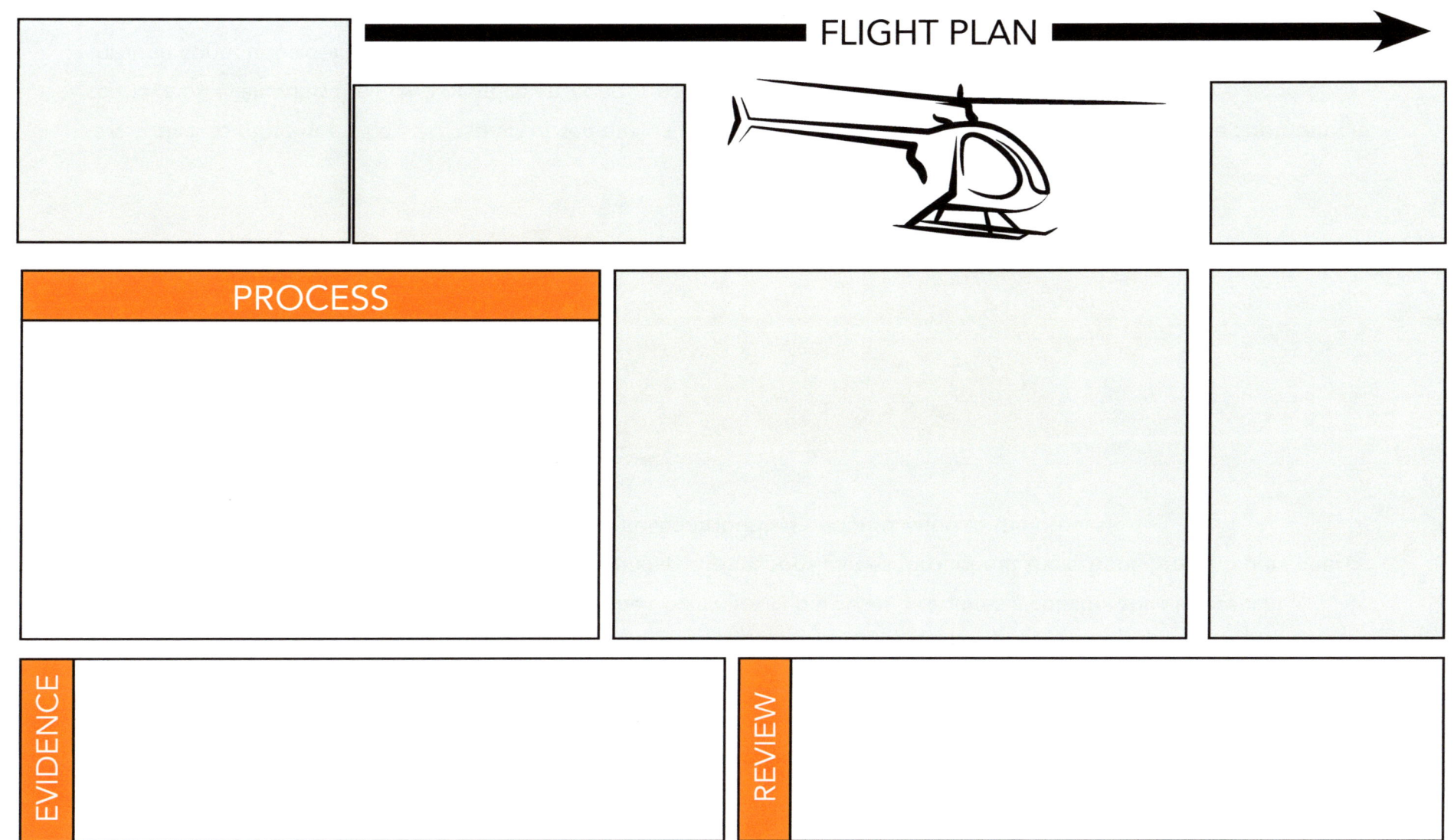

PEOPLE

CHAPTER 4

Roles and self-evaluation

To be truly effective, self-evaluation cannot be owned by one individual or be implemented in pockets or silos by different groups of people, each focusing on their own narrow purpose. It requires a collaborative approach underpinned by trust and the distribution of leadership and responsibilities throughout the school. Stakeholders need to be engaged and encouraged to make meaningful contributions and add value to the process.

> **Every individual in the school has a contribution to make to self-evaluation and everyone should be learning from each other**

It is critical to remember the **self** aspect of self-evaluation, where everyone in the school community has a contribution to make by evaluating their own practice and performance, and by taking personal responsibility for their outcomes through continuous daily improvement. It is not simply about crunching data and measuring the students' academic performance … true self-evaluation is demonstrated through continuous reflective practice at all levels that leads to sustainable improvement in teaching, learning, leadership and management of the school in all areas – students, teachers, parents and the wider school community.

Authentic self-evaluation should be owned and driven by all the school stakeholders. A stakeholder is anyone who can directly or indirectly affect the self-evaluation **process**. It is therefore important for the school's organisational chart and job descriptions to outline responsibilities and accountabilities in relation to self-evaluation. In addition, it is essential for the school's strategy for self-evaluation to show how the different stakeholders should engage with other stakeholders in the process.

For people to be able to engage effectively in a distributed leadership model of self-evaluation, they must first understand and then buy in to the purpose and process. This will require some honest personal evaluation, driven by self-awareness, to help them understand the importance and value of their specific role to the success of the school's self-evaluation. All stakeholders must then have a clear role underpinned by a specific set of responsibilities, expectations and boundaries. These clearly defined roles should provide the framework to accelerate school improvement and effectiveness through appropriate leader behaviour and purposeful interaction with self-evaluation.

ROLE → Responsibilities → Expectations → Boundaries

Responsibilities

People need to know and understand where their responsibilities for self-evaluation begin and end. Individuals need to be clear about the specific tasks they are required to carry out and also how they will be held to account for the outcomes of these activities. When everyone understands and can articulate their personal responsibilities, self-evaluation is likely to have greater cohesion because the **purpose** becomes clearer and the **process** becomes more relevant and manageable to each individual's day to day practice.

Expectations

People need to know precisely what is expected of them with regard to their actions and behaviour to support the school's self-evaluation. Individuals and teams can set targets and measure their own performance in relation to the expectations of their role. The school can build resilience into its self-evaluation process by encouraging people to work together, communicate clear expectations and navigate the challenges through professional collaboration.

Boundaries

People need boundaries to be explicitly defined so that they can see how their role contributes to the overall outcome and how they will be held to account for their performance. Without clear boundaries, some people may overstep their responsibilities causing repetition and unnecessary effort, while others may step back from their tasks or not live up to expectations leading to gaps in the self-evaluation process.

The principal

Each principal will have their preferred approach to self-evaluation, just as they do to other aspects of leadership in the school, but it is important to consider how your own individual style might be perceived by your colleagues and other members of the school community. Some principals may prefer a hands-on approach where they are actively involved in all self-evaluation activities, while others may rely more heavily on delegation through senior and middle leaders. Regardless of your personal style, engaging your people in successful self-evaluation is one of the most important parts of your job as a school leader. The success of your strategy for self-evaluation will therefore depend on developing your people as part of a distributed leadership team who:

> Understand who is responsible for a specific task, and who is accountable for delivering that task.
> Can articulate and deliver expectations around that task.
> Work within agreed boundaries around that task.

Senior and middle leaders

The importance of senior and middle leaders cannot be emphasised enough … they are the agents of effective self-evaluation in any school. They must be able to speak the language of self-evaluation with authenticity, credibility and confidence. Senior leaders need to engage middle leaders in regular systematic discussions to quality assure their work. Maintaining a focus on self-evaluation at these times allows deeper conversations to unpack meaning and explore what lies beneath what the school's leaders are seeing and hearing.

Senior leaders should be able to see the big picture and understand how the evaluation of work in their respective year or phase contributes to the school's overall evaluation of its performance.

Middle leaders should be the powerhouse of knowledge about their respective areas of responsibility and be able to confidently articulate the current position drawn from the different sources of evidence available. In schools where self-evaluation is highly effective, the middle leaders often display a number of traits and characteristics that give them an edge over their counterparts in other schools.

> They understand the strategic purpose of self-evaluation in their school and implement the right activities – at the right time – for the right reasons.

> They analyse and interpret data with a forensic approach to be able to confidently articulate their findings and make relevant decisions for improvement.

> They have a clear schedule and structure to their activities that provide meaningful evaluation in the form of evidence-based portfolios and illustrative examples.

> They integrate and embed self-evaluation activities into their professional practice and constantly check the pulse and monitor the vital signs in their area of responsibility.

> They speak the language of self-evaluation and reinforce this through regular dialogue with their staff colleagues, senior leaders and all school stakeholders.

In schools where self-evaluation is typically viewed as an activity or event prior to an external assessment or inspection, the middle leaders typically keep asking the same question time and time again. This is worrying because it implies that they are not having the right conversations regularly enough through their own work in the school.

What questions will someone be likely to ask me?

If middle leaders are not being asked the right questions by their line managers and senior leaders, they in turn will not be asking the right questions of themselves or their colleagues. This leads to an unhealthy situation where self-evaluation can become unstuck. Therefore, it is essential that all stakeholders in the school engage in regular planned dialogue using the language of self-evaluation. By having these conversations, they will develop greater confidence and credibility to articulate their messages and have a shared understanding of the school's performance.

Put simply, the school's leaders are the glue that holds self-evaluation together. Middle leaders provide stability and structure that allow meaningful activities and conversations to take place at all levels, while senior leaders create a conduit for evidence to flow through the school and for appropriate leadership decisions and actions to be taken.

Language of self-evaluation

One of the most important things for any school to consider is how they will guarantee a common language across all stakeholders involved in the process of self-evaluation. Agreeing clear vocabulary and definitions of terminology will ensure that everyone is working to a standard framework and the possibility of misinterpretation is significantly reduced.

Where do you find your common agreed language?

Having made a clear distinction between school-led self-evaluation and external evaluation, e.g. inspection, this is the point at which the two can usefully converge to provide a ready-made vocabulary. The more your staff, middle leaders, senior leaders and other stakeholders converse among themselves using agreed self-evaluation language, the more comfortable they will be engaging in dialogue with external visitors and authorities.

The language of self-evaluation can be divided into 3 main categories:

1 **Quantifiers**   Provide a clear definition and consistency when describing measurements, such as student progress and quality of teaching.

2 **Technicals**   Provide a clear definition of technical vocabulary, such as a*chievement, attainment, gifted & talented, innovation.*

3 **Descriptors**   Provide a clear definition of terms used to describe and differentiate the judgements in the school's self-evaluation.

It may take time to lay down a glossary of agreed language, but it will be time well spent. This is the foundation on which all your school self-evaluation conversations should take place and it must therefore be solid and secure.

The best way to do this is to refer to rubric in the external evaluation frameworks that are relevant to your school, but here are some examples to get you started:

Quantifiers

What are your school's parameters for these quantifiers?

Quantifiers	Example	Your school's parameters
Almost all	Greater than 90%	
Most	75% - 90%	
Large majority	61% - 74%	
Majority	50% - 60%	
Large minority	31% - 49%	
Minority	16% - 30%	
Few	Up to 15%	

Technicals

How do you define the following terms in your school?

Accountability	Achievement	Accreditation
Age-appropriate	Analysis	Assessment (external)
Assessment (formative)	Assessment (internal)	Assessment (summative)
Attainment	Benchmarking	Best practice
Challenge	Competence	Collaboration
Creative Thinking	Critical Thinking	Data
Differentiate	Engagement	Enquiry
Enrichment	Enterprise	Gifted & Talented
Higher Order Thinking	Inclusion	Independent Learning
Innovation	Interaction	Learning Skills
Logical Thinking	Monitoring	Outcomes
Problem Solving	Progress	Standards
Study Skills	Underachievement	Work Scrutiny

Descriptors

How do you ensure stakeholders are using consistent language to analyse and describe their findings?

Increasing effectiveness

Most	Large majority	Majority	Large minority	Minority	Few
Better than expected		Expected		Less than expected	
Consistently		Frequently		Usually	Rarely
Expertly	Effectively	Consistently	Securely	Regularly	Inconsistently
Rigorously		Effectively		Appropriately	
Rigorous		Regular		Periodic	
Highly successful	Very successful	Successful		Adequate	Inadequate
Strategic		Operational			
Systematic		Planned		Inconsistent	
Fully embedded		Embedded		Fragmented	
All levels		Some levels		Individual	

Giving self-evaluation a voice

It is important to give self-evaluation a voice by encouraging all stakeholders to engage in dialogue at the right time, in the right place and for the right purpose. This will contribute to the authenticity of the school's self-evaluation.

Students are your most important stakeholders and the reason your school exists. When self-evaluation is fully embedded and integrated into the life of a school, it is highly visible in the learning environment and permeates the day-to-day conversations that take place. Students form the foundation for this, during their interactions in lessons and other activities. They should be able to evaluate their own performance based on their starting points in relation to the expectations of their performance within a subject, group, or team. Your students' knowledge and understanding of where they stand, what is next and how they are going to bridge the gaps and extend their learning is essential to support student attainment and progress in your school's self-evaluation.

Students can reinforce their contribution through the language they use when doing self and peer reviews of their learning, and engagements such as student voice, forums and school councils give rich opportunities to collect valuable evidence on their views. Regularly engaging your students' voice is the best way to monitor whether your **strategy** for self-evaluation is working or not. Their voices help you see the big picture so that you can make adjustments, as needed. Your students' active reflection and participation ensures that the **purpose** and **process** of self-evaluation is making an impact.

Parents believe in your school's vision and trust your staff to deliver on its promises. Their voice, whether positive or negative, alerts you to what is working and what is not. How your school engages with parents and responds to their voice is critical to your self-evaluation and your school's effectiveness. The parent-school relationship requires open mindedness, trust and honesty. Parents are the school's greatest advocates, for good or bad, and are a source of expertise in the community. Therefore, actively engaging parents ensures that your self-evaluation is fit for purpose. Parents provide a rich source of communication for self-evaluation. Whether through formal surveys, working groups, consultation evenings with teachers or informal gatherings, the school can gain valuable insights by keeping a focus on self-evaluation during these events.

Governors must hold the principal to account for the school's performance, through agreed targets and metrics, and should be engaging with self-evaluation in all their dealings with the school. Governors should be able to articulate the big picture and understand how their ability to hold the school to account impacts the effectiveness of the school's **strategy** for self-evaluation.

Teachers have the most direct relationship with the students and their parents in the school. They should also be able to see the big picture and understand how the evaluation of learning in their respective classes contributes to the school's overall evaluation of its performance, as well as contributing to the evaluation of relevant themes arising from the leadership decisions taken in the school. Teachers start with a blank canvas in their classrooms and, with a little thought, can engage students and use displays to provide a learning environment that creates visible and explicit opportunities for self-evaluation.

Support staff are responsible for carrying out operational duties, including one-to-one support of students as delegated by teachers. They should also be able to see the big picture and understand how the evaluation of their own performance in relation to their responsibilities contributes to the school's overall evaluation of its performance.

Everyone in the school community has a contribution to make, and a role to play, in self-evaluation. Once everyone is aware of, and understands, their unique contribution through the school's strategy for self-evaluation, they can take personal and collective responsibility for their part by taking appropriate actions.

Connecting your people so that they understand their individual impact on the school's outcomes will help develop authentic and connected relationships between your different stakeholders. Meaningful and purposeful discussions between different stakeholders will raise awareness and drive individual and group behaviour and actions. These collective actions, coupled with a robust and coherent **strategy** for self-evaluation, will **accelerate** the school's improvement ensuring progress towards the intended outcomes for students.

How do you currently ensure that all stakeholders are involved in giving self-evaluation a voice?

How people behave towards self-evaluation

Sometimes things flow smoothly and everyone is happy and productive with the results of their actions. Yet at other times, the same people hit barriers, and the issues that are raised colour the way they feel and behave. This means that principals not only need to be aware of the different ways their behaviour impacts the school's stakeholders but to also know how to intervene when the behaviour of others impacts the school's progress and ultimately, the speed and effectiveness of their self-evaluation efforts.

We are introducing a series of fun and friendly characters to help illustrate the continuum of behaviour patterns that we have observed when focusing on self-evaluation in schools.

It is natural and human to adopt any of these behaviours at different times in the school's schedule or year. Being self-aware, and having the ability to see your own actions and how they impact others, is the first step to taking personal responsibility for your behaviour. Open, honest and transparent communication with stakeholders about how they are behaving and impacting self-evaluation will help stakeholders remove barriers and find better ways of working together.

Planning and approach

The turtle and the owl characterise the continuum of behaviours in relation to the **purpose** of self-evaluation and typically adopt different ways of planning and approaching self-evaluation.

Passive
Random
Reactive
Compliance-led
Narrow focus

Planning
&
Approach

Active
Specific
Proactive
School-led
360 degree view

Turtle behaviour

If people don't like what they see, they may decide to retreat back into their shell for a period of time. Behaving like a turtle provides an opportunity for self-reflection but is often characterised by withdrawing from active participation in the self-evaluation process. This behaviour is not sustainable and will eventually lead to a breakdown in relationships and trust in the school community.

The need for a period of self-reflection can happen at any stage in an individual's career and is often triggered by external factors, such as inspection, validation and accreditation visits, changes in senior staffing and/or change of school. Withdrawing from active participation in the self-evaluation process may meet an individual's short-term personal needs but it creates professional uncertainty and vulnerability. This approach is uncomfortable for everyone concerned and it is imperative that retreating from active duty is not tolerated for extended periods of time.

What is the impact? When individuals withdraw from participation in the **process**, a number of things are likely to start happening that will have a negative impact on the effectiveness of the school's self-evaluation. Individual leaders may sustain their own roles and responsibilities but, without everyone's active contribution, they are unlikely to make meaningful connections between all the school's activities. If it is the principal or another senior leader that manifests turtle behaviour – this is a serious weakness and the school is in trouble.

What can the principal do? When people retreat from participation, the principal needs to intervene, determine the cause and then follow up with strong clear direction and articulation of responsibilities, expectations and boundaries.

Owl behaviour

When people adopt owl behaviour, they understand the purpose of self-evaluation and know how they are expected to contribute to the bigger picture of evaluating the school's performance. They can see how the process aligns with overall improvement in the school, but this can also mean that they become distracted and spend time focusing on things that may not be immediately relevant to their own work or area of responsibility.

Behaving as the all-seeing owl helps people to realise the importance of getting as broad a picture as possible of their performance and start to develop a 360-degree view of what is really happening. When people behave in this way, they require joined-up thinking and processes with clear lines of accountability to make sure that their contribution to self-evaluation is relevant.

What is the impact? The principal and senior leaders have to work together to define a clear purpose then establish clear lines of accountability for the implementation of self-evaluation. To do this, they need to remove themselves from the practical implementation of the self-evaluation process and trust the middle leaders and staff to get on with the job. By stepping back from the detail, they are more likely to see the bigger picture and have a better understanding of what is actually happening in the school. However, there is still the inherent danger that self-evaluation lacks rigour because – despite the depth of internal evidence and evaluation this behaviour is likely to produce – there is a lack of an external perspective of the school's performance.

Who can the principal do? When the principal works in collaboration with senior leaders to determine the focus, this can lead to wiser decision-making and planning across the school. These leaders need to be held accountable to manage and oversee a broad base of evidence for self-evaluation which, in turn, requires them to develop distributed leadership and bring the school's middle leaders and other stakeholders into the process.

Evidence and rigour

The caterpillar and the wolf characterise the continuum of behaviours in relation to the **process** and typically adopt different ways of implementing self-evaluation.

Weak
Generalised
Internal
Narrow focus
Unbalanced view

Evidence & Rigour

Strong
Evidence driven
Internal and external
Constant scanning
Balanced view

Caterpillar behaviour

When people exist too comfortably in their own environment, and only focus on what is happening around them at that point in time, they are unable to see what is happening elsewhere or what the future holds. By behaving like a caterpillar towards self-evaluation, individual staff may have an understanding of what is working in their immediate areas of responsibility, but they are unlikely to volunteer information or stray outside their comfort zone.

If too many people are narrowly focussed on their own area of responsibility, self-evaluation will still take place but it is likely to be fragmented with a lack of purpose. People carry out the process and produce evidence that is not shared in any meaningful way. Decisions are not based on secure evidence, relationships become strained and trust starts to break down. The danger of behaving in this way for any length of time is that these key weaknesses will eventually be exposed and the school's leadership, and subsequent self-evaluation, will suffer.

What is the impact? The process is carried out but with little clarity or purpose. A lot of time, energy and effort can be wasted because everything becomes fragmented and reactive to individual situations. As a result, the school is vulnerable.

What can the principal do? The principal needs to ensure that the school's culture and work environment supports authentic self-evaluation. Sometimes, the principal will need to dictate the focus to some members of staff to be perceived as taking ownership of the school's performance, otherwise self-evaluation will be driven by the separate agendas of the individual staff.

Wolf behaviour

When people adopt wolf behaviour, they are comfortable enough to step outside their immediate environment and gain an external perspective of their performance. By behaving in this way, people scan the external environment and develop a much richer perspective and understanding of what is happening around them. Adopting wolf behaviour means that individuals get a more balanced view to support the evaluation of the school's performance.

What is the impact? This approach requires the principal to manage a new level of oversight where they encourage everyone to constantly review the school's performance against external factors and scan for potential threats and weaknesses. When this works well, the school has a much more rounded view of its performance and all staff are better informed to make decisions relevant to their role and area of responsibility. However, individuals need to make sure that they don't become distracted by too many external initiatives and irrelevant evidence. There also needs to be a high level of trust, otherwise staff can become suspicious of their leaders' motives and this can lead to the perception of a predator/prey relationship in the school. If this happens then self-evaluation becomes a threat rather than a meaningful process to support the school.

What can the principal do? The principal needs to adopt wolf behaviour to obtain a more secure foundation on which to establish evidence-based decisions and actions. It is critical for the principal to communicate clearly and allay any fears and suspicions about the motive and purpose of self-evaluation. They therefore need to set the agenda and work with senior leaders to ensure the most relevant internal and external sources of evidence are used to focus the school's self-evaluation process.

Resources and allocation

The ninja and the bee characterise the continuum of behaviours in relation to the engagement and involvement of **people** in self-evaluation and typically adopt different ways of using people as a resource.

Ninja behaviour

When people adopt ninja behaviour they take on the mantle and personal responsibility of self-evaluation. They start to believe they have to do everything themselves if they want to achieve results. This type of behaviour means that people are energised and get things done, but it is also dangerous because it can create fractures in the school and affect its capacity to improve.

What is the impact? People may consider that they are being thorough, analytical and have taken responsibility for finding things out for themselves … but in reality … this behaviour can often be perceived as an aggressive warrior-like stance to self-evaluation. Consequently, the self-evaluation process becomes a compliance approach with checklists and quotas. Ultimately, this can demotivate their colleagues and performance will suffer. In addition, this behaviour typically divides the senior leadership team and creates fractures in the school's capacity to improve. There is nothing more dangerous than people who try to 'go it alone' and start to believe their own hype! This behaviour can create a clear danger to the sustainability of meaningful self-evaluation in a school.

What can the principal do? The ninja approach to self-evaluation is characterised by individuals assuming the belief that they have the power to fix everything but have to do it alone. Typically, this means they continue to isolate themselves from other staff and are often perceived as taking action without any clear rationale or purpose. The focus for self-evaluation is therefore unclear and inconsistent across the school. Therefore, the principal must keep lines of communication clear and ensure that all stakeholders understand their purpose and role in self-evaluation.

Bee behaviour

When people adopt purposeful busy bee behaviour, they are visibly collecting as much evidence as possible, checking in with different stakeholders and working with the senior leadership team to collate and analyse results with a specific purpose leading towards an intended outcome. Self-evaluation processes include a variety of planned activities focussed on a specific goal. Staff are involved in cycles of lesson observations, work scrutiny, data analysis and other monitoring activities with meaning and purpose through ongoing and continuous feedback and review loops.

What is the impact? Planned and purposeful self-evaluation activities allocate resources on the specific areas of the school requiring attention and improvement. Staff become meaningfully involved in a continuous cycle of reflection with a clear agenda and direction for improvement planning which is articulated and understood by all. Consequently, the self-evaluation process becomes a school-led approach backed by rigorous, quality assured evidence.

Who can the principal do? The principal needs to proactively allocate staff and resources to the school's strategy for self-evaluation. By distributing leadership roles and holding people to account on a school-led agenda for school improvement, authentic self-evaluation will lead to accelerated student outcomes and school performance.

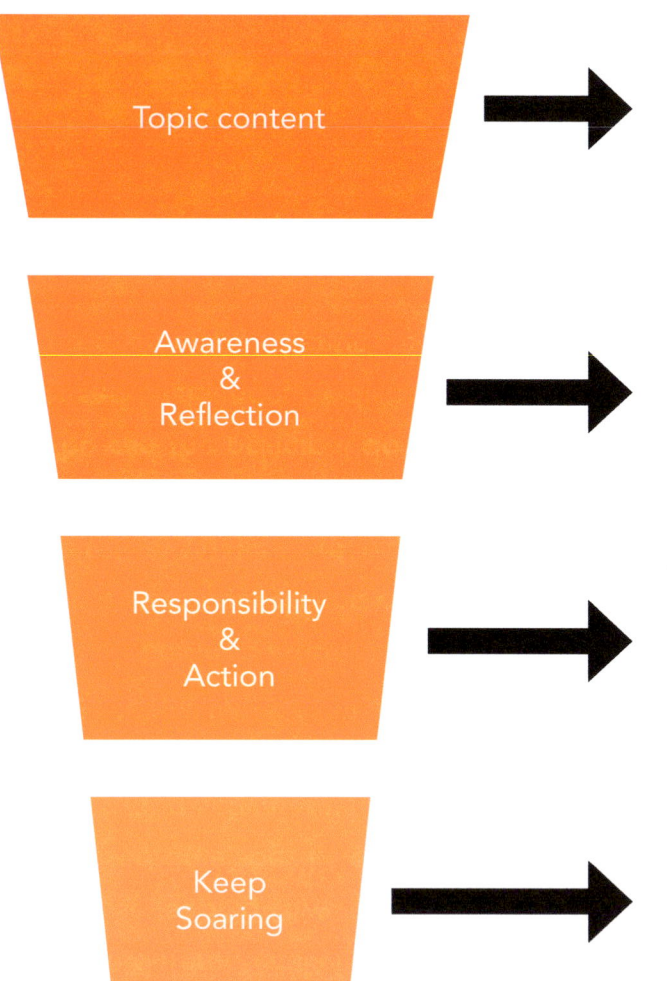

In this chapter, we have focused on the school's **people** and the need to engage all stakeholders in the purpose and process of your school's self-evaluation. We have identified the importance of defining clear roles (responsibilities, expectations, boundaries) and accountability, and considered how people may behave differently at different times. We have also stressed the importance of having an agreed shared vocabulary to allow meaningful dialogue to take place.

The key questions on the following pages should help you to reflect and articulate the current situation, with regard to the **people** involved in self-evaluation in your school.

Taking the main messages from this chapter, and the outcomes from your reflection, use the NOTES page to identify what needs to happen next and how this will be implemented to strengthen the **people** aspect of your school's self-evaluation.

Using the **same leadership decision** from the previous chapters, complete the highlighted sections on the Keep Soaring flight plan on page 120.

PEOPLE: KEY INSIGHTS

How are the different stakeholders behaving towards the PURPOSE of self-evaluation in your school?

How are the different stakeholders interacting with the other different PEOPLE responsible for self-evaluation?

What impact is the behaviour of different stakeholders having on the PROCESS of self-evaluation?

What are the roles of different stakeholder groups in relation to self-evaluation in your school? Use the table on the next page to identify their respective responsibilities, expectations and boundaries.

Stakeholder	Role	Responsibilities	Expectations	Boundaries
Principal				
Senior Leaders				
Middle Leaders				
Teachers				
Support Staff				
Students				
Parents				
Governors				
Other				

NOTES

FLIGHT PLAN

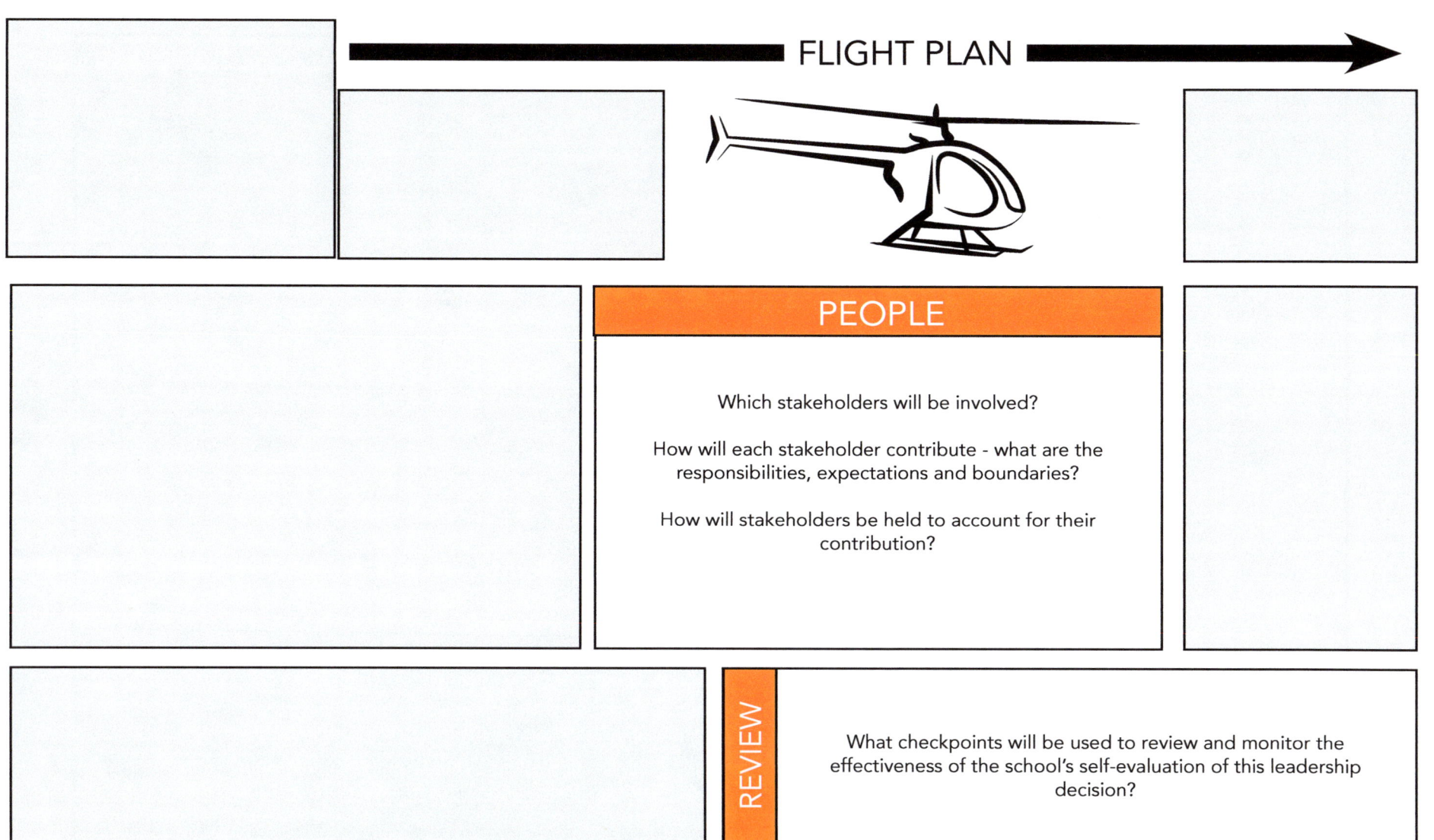

PEOPLE

Which stakeholders will be involved?

How will each stakeholder contribute - what are the responsibilities, expectations and boundaries?

How will stakeholders be held to account for their contribution?

REVIEW

What checkpoints will be used to review and monitor the effectiveness of the school's self-evaluation of this leadership decision?

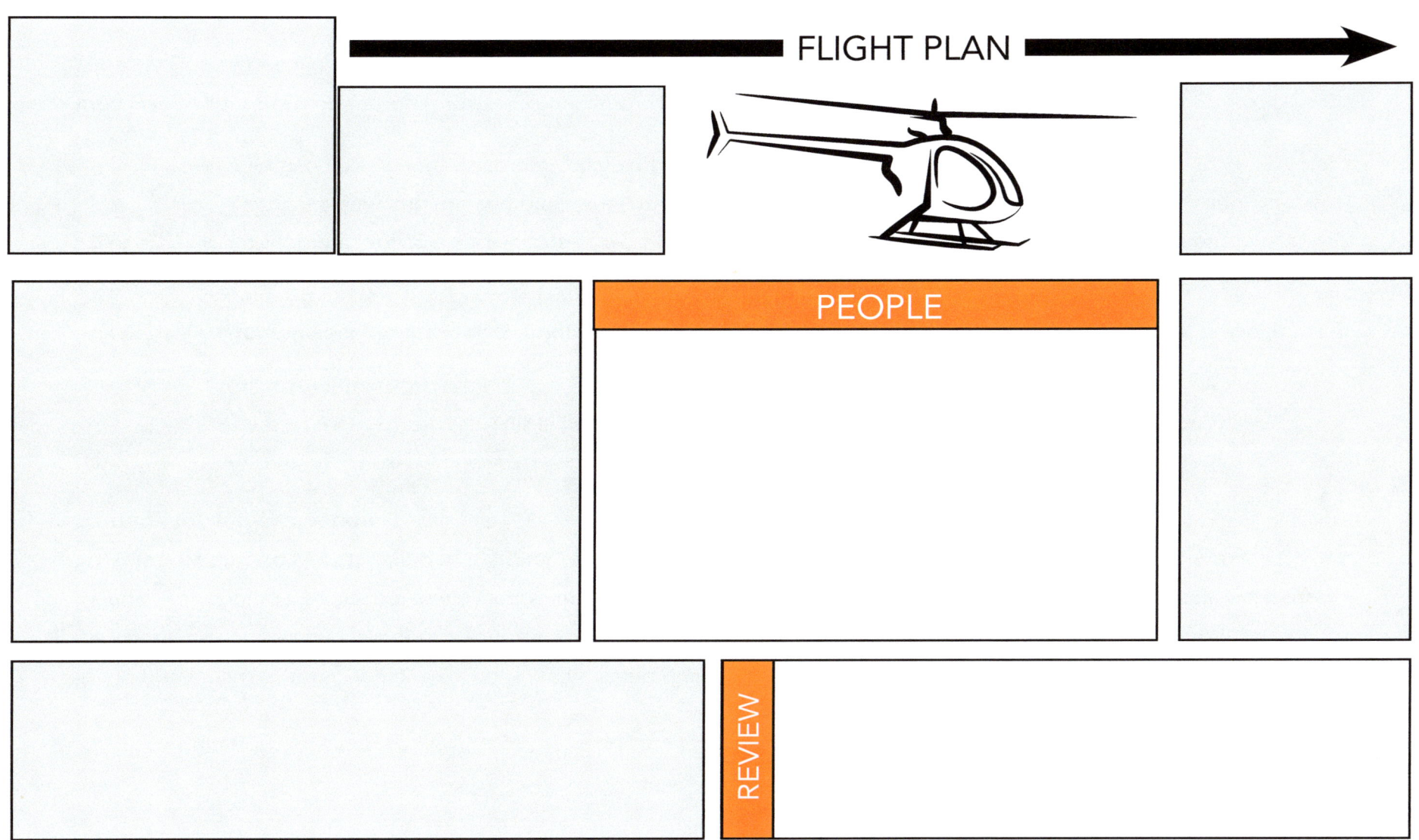

FLIGHT PLAN

PEOPLE

REVIEW

120

KEEP SOARING

CHAPTER 5

Strategy and all things strategic

In the previous chapters, we have asked questions and guided you to reflect on your current practice. At times, this may have challenged and disrupted your thinking, but you should have identified what is working well in your school. By now, you should also have a much clearer understanding of what needs to change in relation to your self-evaluation. So, it is now time to start thinking at a higher level and consider what this means for your school in relation to a **strategy for self-evaluation**

Operational   An outline of what you will focus on for the near future, with details of activity, timescales and measurement of results. This is typically your annual school improvement plan supported by faculty, departmental, subject or phase/grade action plans.

Strategic   An outline of your mission, vision and high-level goals, and the projects required to achieve these, for the next 3-5 years. This is typically your school's strategic plan.

Strategy   A blueprint for achieving success over a period of time, with a clearly defined purpose and outcomes. This is typically the missing piece that integrates your self-evaluation to measure the impact and effectiveness of your decisions, planning and actions for improvement.

One way to shift from operational ❯ strategic ❯ strategy is to imagine that you are moving through different levels to widen your perspective.

Get off the train

At this level, the principal typically becomes bogged down in detail and implementation. Self-evaluation systems and processes may be clearly defined and embedded into the life of the school but, just like a train, movement is tightly controlled and can only happen in one direction at a time. This is a one-size fits all approach, without regard to the school's context, and is highly operational. It is characterised by an over-reliance on structure and a tightly defined framework of processes, while neglecting the individual and collective strengths/weaknesses of the people responsible for carrying out the self-evaluation process in the school.

PURPOSE — Complete a linear sequence of activities and travel in one direction with a predetermined end point.

PROCESS — Pre-defined and inflexible because a train can only travel on the tracks that are laid down.

PEOPLE — Driven and steered by one individual. Stakeholders may have a good view from the windows but will only see what is in the immediate vicinity and may therefore miss something important.

Get out of the balloon

At this next level, the principal is aware of the need to rise above the detail and get a wider view of the school and its performance. Self-evaluation is broadened to include external analysis of performance but lacks evidence of impact. This broader perspective typically supports a school to develop and achieve a judgement of 'good' but it also creates a ceiling through which the school is likely to struggle to improve its effectiveness further. There is an increasing degree of freedom of movement requiring greater flexibility in how people behave. However, this freedom is also influenced by external factors, which can disrupt alignment between purpose and process.

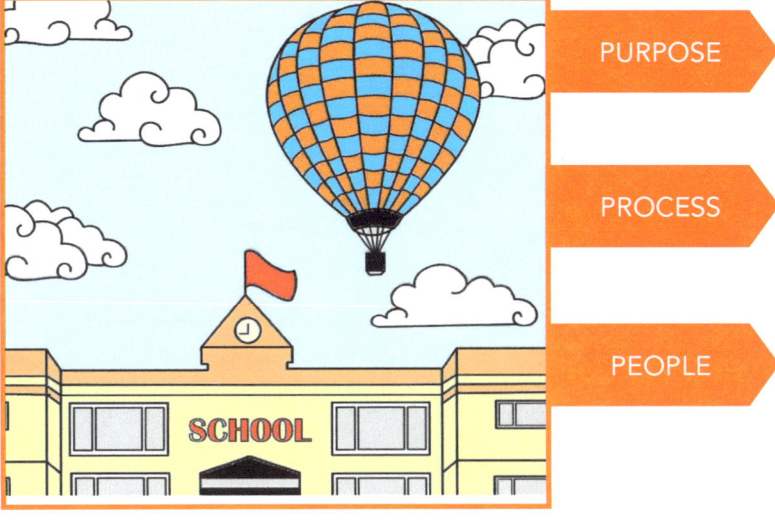

PURPOSE
Gain a wider view but this lacks directionality and is at the mercy of external factors.

PROCESS
Combination of internal data and external perspective provides a more balanced analysis.

PEOPLE
Distributed leadership – a balloon is a complex dynamic system that needs a team to launch and maintain it during flight.

Get into the helicopter

It is no coincidence that this book is titled KEEP SOARING. The ultimate approach for any principal is to soar above the minutia and achieve a helicopter view of the school and its performance. This is supported by developing an evidence-based school-led strategy for self-evaluation that achieves a three-dimensional analysis of the school, taking the maximum range of relevant internal and external evidence into account. It is only by getting this full aerial perspective that you can truly understand all the factors and influences for you school and ensure that your self-evaluation is authentic.

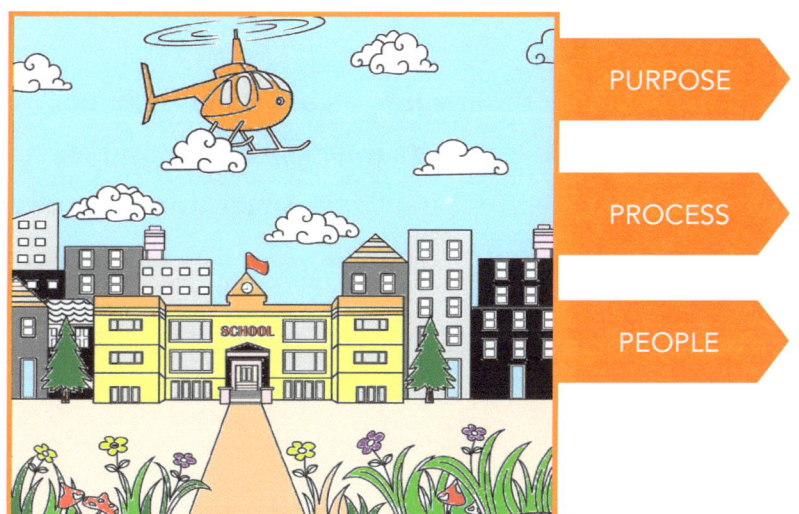

PURPOSE — High level aerial view with flexibility and maneouverability to change pace and direction.

PROCESS — Big picture with overview of all connected activities.

PEOPLE — Helicopters are highly complex machines and require carefully scheduled attention by teams of committed individuals to keep them functioning smoothly.

Keep Soaring

One key advantage of a helicopter is its ability to move in multiple dimensions. It can hover and focus when needed, can pitch forward for a more precise view, can accelerate forward or backward, can yaw left and right, and can also move up and down to broaden and narrow the horizon in all directions. Therefore, by maintaining a high-level view from the cockpit, a principal will have the capacity to make sure that the school's self-evaluation activity is responsive, relevant and **fit for purpose** at all times.

Helicopters can take off quickly and navigate in diverse environments. When this flexibility and manoeuvrability is aligned to a clear flight plan (strategy), the school will be in a prime position to ensure that its self-evaluation informs improvement planning and drives continuous improvement in the areas that really matter.

Staying in your helicopter will provide an opportunity to combine vision and action. It will help you to keep an overview of what is happening in your immediate vicinity, without having to stay too close to the detail, and will also make it easier for you to see and navigate the route ahead. The aerial perspective will allow you to scan for any potential factors that may influence your self-evaluation journey and will ultimately support the school in closing the gap between where you are now and where you want to be.

Flying a helicopter is an exhilarating experience … so grab your wings and let's **keep soaring**.

Developing your strategy

Your school's strategy for self-evaluation is probably one of the most important documents you will put together. It should be the blueprint for measuring and evaluating the school's development and should allow you to articulate and communicate this in a simple way to all stakeholders.

> **A clearly defined well-structured strategy for self-evaluation should provide the blueprint to support and drive the school's future improvement**

The whole purpose of creating a strategy for self-evaluation is to help you clarify your school improvement activities and create a focused flow that drives the implementation and integration of your self-evaluation process. Stop using someone else's strategy (inspectors, regulators, external authorities) to drive **your** school's self-evaluation. Instead, start creating an authentic **evidence-based school-led strategy** for self-evaluation that is specific to your school.

Self-evaluation strategy

When you have a self-evaluation strategy, you have an understanding of what self-evaluation should look like and use it as one of the management tools in your school.

This approach puts the emphasis on self-evaluation as a process that you know has to take place but can ultimately lead to evaluation for the sake of evaluation. It typically creates lots of activity but can often lack focus and purpose.

Micro self-evaluation

Strategic self-evaluation

When self-evaluation is implemented strategically, it is driven by the goals and objectives in the school improvement plan, which means that you know the areas of the school where your attention needs to be focussed.

This approach can result in a lot of data and evidence on the school's key areas for improvement, but often narrows the focus to academic performance to the detriment of other aspects of students' learning.

Macro self-evaluation

Strategy for self-evaluation

When you create a strategy for self-evaluation, your purpose is to show that there has been a demonstrable impact resulting from the decisions and actions taken in the school.

This approach focuses on the analysis of quality evidence from the broad range of stakeholders to accurately evaluate how well the people and process have strengthened improvement planning and improved students' learning outcomes (purpose).

Means end self-evaluation

127

By working through the previous chapters in this book, and answering the key questions at the end of each section, you should have reflected on your current practice and already have identified some potential actions to integrate into the school's approach to self-evaluation. The next step is to focus on the strategy as a method of aligning the **purpose** with the **process** and **people** in your school.

It is now time to bring everything together and to create your strategy by considering why you are engaging in self-evaluation (purpose), what you are doing to achieve this (process) and who needs to be involved (people).

Remember that you are not trying to produce a detailed operational plan – this should sit elsewhere in your school's planning systems.

You are aiming to organise your thoughts and create a flight plan to ensure that the school is doing the right things for the right reasons at the right time, rather than simply for the sake of engaging in self-evaluation.

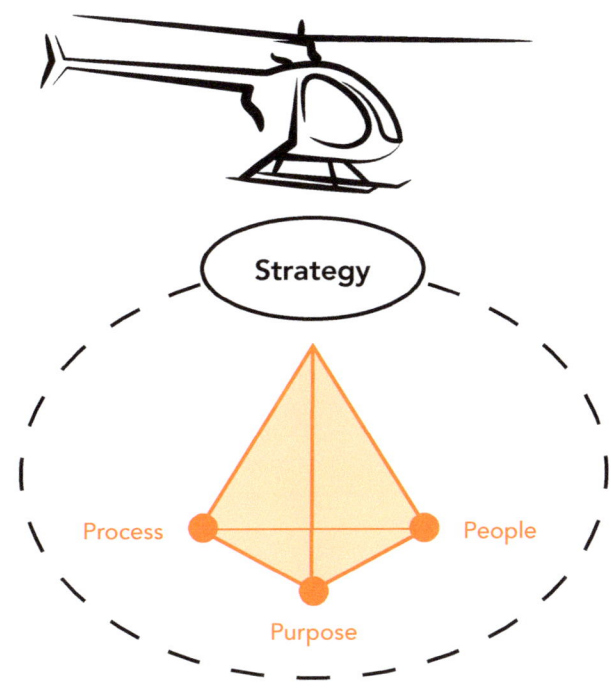

Your **strategy** (flight plans) should align and integrate the **purpose, process** and **people** to ensure that the school's leadership decisions are evaluated in terms of their **impact** measured by the improvement on student outcomes. It should also ensure that subsequent actions are **school-led** arising from **evidence-based** decisions, relevant to the **context** of your school.

By working through the individual chapters on **purpose**, **process** and **people**, you should already have started to build up your flight plan for a single leadership decision in your school on pages 54, 90 and 120.

Use the blank template to bring these individual elements together and create your strategy for the evaluation of this trail in your school. You should then have a clearly defined **strategy** for the self-evaluation of this **single** improvement focus to assist in communication with the relevant stakeholders.

We suggest that you use (and adapt where necessary) this template to produce a single page flight plan that outlines the strategy and drives self-evaluation for **each** of the leadership decisions that are relevant to your school.

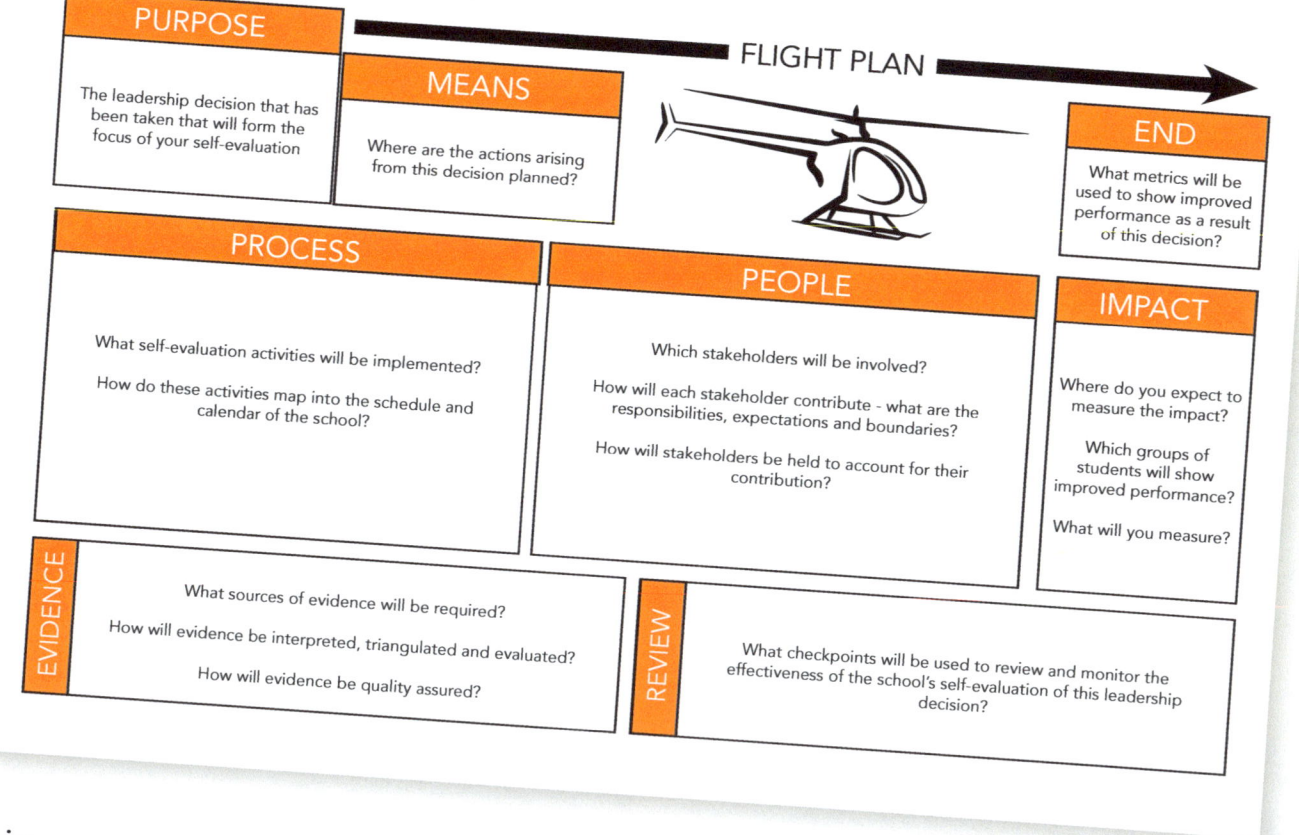

PURPOSE

The leadership decision that has been taken that will form the focus of your self-evaluation

MEANS

Where are the actions arising from this decision planned?

FLIGHT PLAN

END

What metrics will be used to show improved performance as a result of this decision?

PROCESS

What self-evaluation activities will be implemented?

How do these activities map into the schedule and calendar of the school?

PEOPLE

Which stakeholders will be involved?

How will each stakeholder contribute - what are the responsibilities, expectations and boundaries?

How will stakeholders be held to account for their contribution?

IMPACT

Where do you expect to measure the impact?

Which groups of students will show improved performance?

What will you measure?

EVIDENCE

What sources of evidence will be required?

How will evidence be interpreted, triangulated and evaluated?

How will evidence be quality assured?

REVIEW

What checkpoints will be used to review and monitor the effectiveness of the school's self-evaluation of this leadership decision?

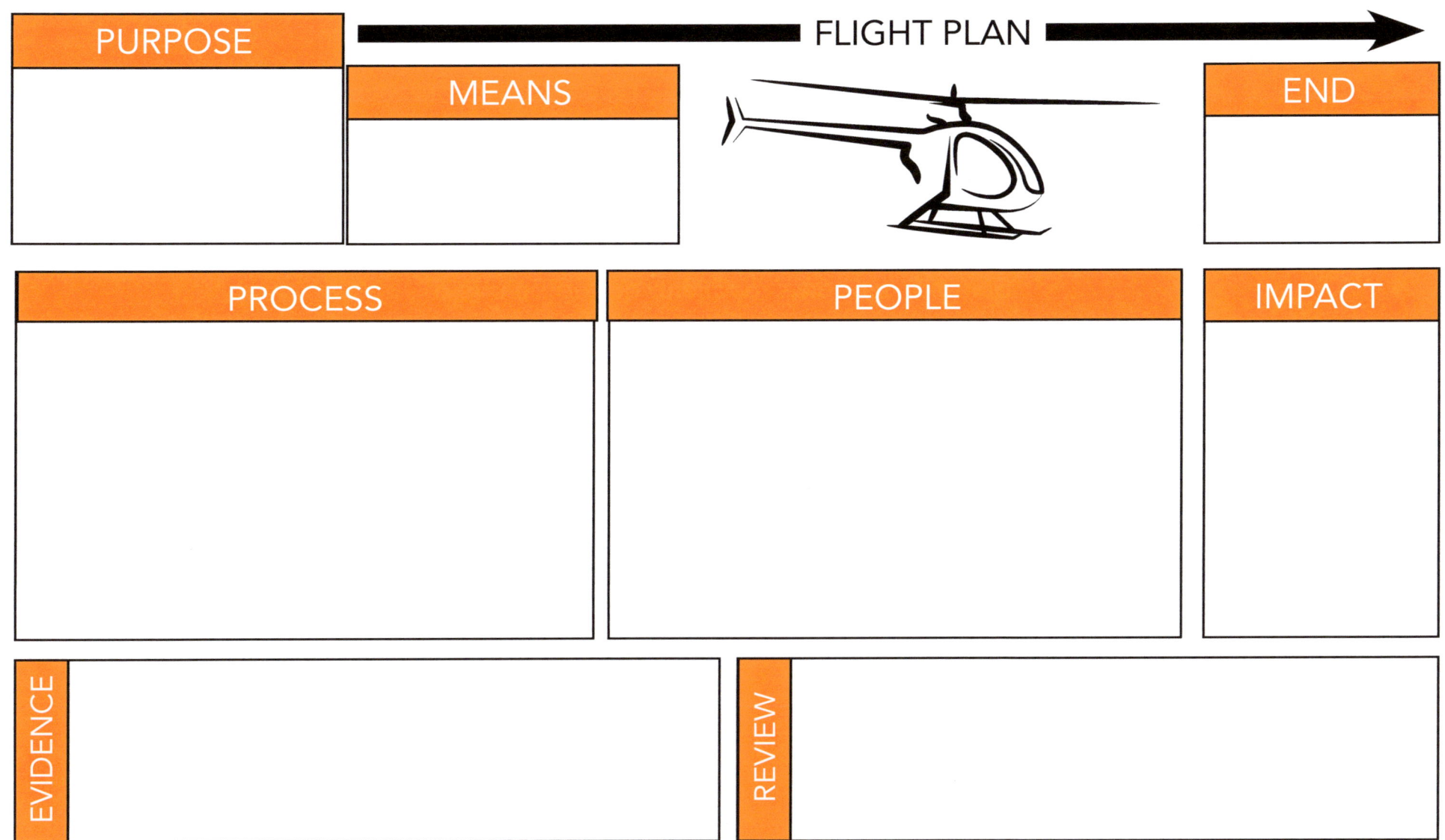

Keep Soaring

Focus on the leadership and management decisions being taken to drive the school's improvement planning

Define your decisions and actions in the context of your school

Identify the key evaluation trails relevant to your school

Collect the right evidence at the right time for the right reasons

Evaluate the impact of the school's improvement planning on the quality of students' learning

Determine how well the school's self-evaluation has supported and strengthened improvement and what needs to be done differently

School-led

Evidence-based

Authentic

Lesley Hunter

Lesley is an internationally recognised speaker and consultant specialising in developing leaders to deliver outstanding performance. She is a former lead inspector and has worked with schools across all phases of education in Europe and the Middle East. Her recent work at government level has supported the strategic introduction and quality assurance of a national educational reform programme for moral education in the United Arab Emirates. Lesley is the author of a series of leadership books and is an adjunct professor and guest lecturer on MBA and MSc courses in several international universities. Her doctorate established a behavioural framework to support the development of effective leaders for the 21st century and this research is continuing through a global project focusing on the authentic behaviour of senior leaders in schools.

Maggie Wright

Maggie is a passionate educator committed to life-long learning and personal development. A senior executive leader, with global international experience, she works collaboratively to ensure outstanding learning outcomes for all students and staff. Maggie has a strategic approach to self-evaluation, leader development at all levels, and school improvement. Her authentic leadership has delivered positive outcomes in diverse and complex multi-lingual school environments in North America, South America, Europe, Asia and the Middle East. Maggie is an outgoing fun-loving person with strong, yet flexible, views and a genuine compassion for others. Driven by vision and purpose, she is keen to achieve success for all. Maggie's doctoral research focuses on how schools accelerate improvement through authentic self-evaluation.

"Keep Soaring is a one of a kind book that every school leader should be dying to get their hands on. At last, a comprehensive overview of school self-evaluation that moves effortlessly from the theoretical to the practical, allowing the reader to develop a deep understanding, with opportunities to reflect on implications within one's own school environment. Broken down into the key elements that constitute outstanding self-evaluative practice, the book presents the reader with an opportunity to develop a comprehensive skill set - each area building on previous areas and leading into deeper, more meaningful processes. Whilst rooted in research and evidence, the book is ultimately a practical guide with theoretical underpinning, that is, importantly, loads of fun to work through."

Brendon Fulton (Principal), 'Outstanding' Dubai British School

FURTHER READING

School self-evaluation: STRATEGY

Baars, S., Bernardes, E., Elwick, A., Malorie, A., McAleavy, T., McInerney, L., Menzies, L., Riggal, A. (2014). Lessons from London Schools: Investigating the Success. Reading: CfBT Education Trust.

Chapman, C., Sammons, P. (2013). School Self-Evaluation for School Improvement: What works and why? Reading: CfBT Education Trust.

O'Brien, S., McNamara, G., O'Hara, J. (2014). Critical facilitators: External supports for self-evaluation and improvement in schools. Studies in Educational Evaluation, 43, 169-177.

OECD. (2013). Synergies for Better Learning: An international perspective on evaluation and assessment. OECD Reviews of Evaluation and Assessment in Education. Paris: OECD Publishing.

McAleavey, T., Riggal, A. (2017). The rapid improvement of government schools in England. Reading: Education Development Trust.

Ryan, K., Gandha, T., Ahn, J. (2013). School Self-Evaluation and Inspection for Improving U.S. Schools? Boulder: National Educational Policy Center (NEPC).

School self-evaluation: PURPOSE

Chapman, C., Sammons, P. (2013). School Self-Evaluation for School Improvement: What works and why? Reading: CfBT Education Trust.

Dimeck, A.M. (2006). Improvement Through Evaluation: Exploring the self-evaluation processes used by a sample of schools. Nottingham: National College for School Leadership. Dunford and MacBeath 2005

Faubert, V. (2009). School evaluation: current practices in OECD countries and a literature review. OECD Education Working Papers, No. 42, Paris: OECD Publishing.

Leung, C. (2005) Accountability versus school development: Self-evaluation in an international school in Hong Kong. International Studies in Educational Administration, 33, 1, 2005.

MacBeath, J. (2005b). School Self-evaluation: Background, Principles and Key Learning. Nottingham: National College of School Leadership.

Matthias, C. (2012). Investigating the school improvement needs and practices of London Primary and Secondary Schools. BMG Research Report, DFE – RR244

McAleavey, T., Riggal, A. (2017). The rapid improvement of government schools in England. Reading: Education Development Trust.

NCSL. (2012). School self-evaluation: Thinkpiece. Level 2. Nottingham: National College for School Leadership.

Ofsted. (2006). Best Practice in Self-Evaluation: a survey of schools, colleges and local authorities.

Thornley, T. (2012). Purpose, principles and focus of school evaluation: Opinion piece. National College for School Leadership.

United Arab Emirates School Inspection Framework. (2015). Dubai: KHDA.

School self-evaluation: PEOPLE

Avolio, B., Gardner, W., Walumbwa, F., Luthans, F., May, D. (2004). Unlocking the mask: a look at the process by which authentic leaders impact follower attitudes and behaviours. The Leadership Quarterly, 15, 6, 801- 823.

Behnke, K., Steins, G. (2017). Principals' reactions to feedback received by school inspection: A longitudinal study. Journal of Educational Change, 17, 77-106

Fox, J., Gong, T., Attoh, P. (2015). The impact of principal as authentic leader of on teacher trust in the K-12 educational context. Journal of Leadership Studies, 8, 4, 6-18.

Hargreaves, D. (2010). Creating a self-improving school system. Nottingham: National College for Leadership of Schools and Children's Services, Schools and Academies.

Hargreaves, D. (2011). Leading a self-improving system: Thinkpiece. Nottingham: National College for School Leadership.

Hargreaves, A., Boyle, A., Harris, A. (2014). Uplifting Leadership: How Organizations, Teams and Communities Raise Performance. San Francisco: Jossey-Bass.

Hargreaves, A. Shirley, D. (2018). Leading from the Middle: Spreading Learning, Well-being and Identity Across Ontario. Ontario: CODE Consortium.

Hofman, R., Dijkstra, N., Hofman, A. (2009). School self-evaluation and student achievement, School Effectiveness and School Improvement, 20, 1, 47-68.

Hopkins, E., Hendry, H., Garrod, F., McClare, S., Pettit, D., Smith, L., Burrell, H., Temple, J. (2016). Teachers' views of the impact of school evaluation and external inspection processes. Improving Schools, 19, 1, 52-61.

Hunter, L. (2018). Challenge Choice Change: How to be a better leader in 18 days. UK: Pack Leader Publications.

Leduc, C., Bouffard, T. (2017). The impact of biased self-evaluations of school and social competence on academic and social functioning. Learning and Individual Differences, 55, 193-201.

MacBeath, J. (2008). Leading learning in the self-evaluating school. School Leadership and Management, 28, 4, 385-399.

Penninckx, M. (2017). Effects and side effects of school inspections: A general framework. Studies in Educational Evaluation, 52, 1-11.

Pink, D. (2009). Drive: The surprising truth about what motivates us. Edinburgh: Canongate Books.

Plowright, D., Godfrey, R. (2008). School self-evaluation: Can head teachers meet the new challenge? International Studies in Educational Administration, 36, 3, 35-59.

Vanhoof, J., Van Petegem, P. (2010). Evaluation the quality of self-evaluation: The (mis)match between internal and external meta-evaluation. Studies in Education Evaluation, 36, 20-26.

Vanhoof, J. Van Petegem, P., DeMaeyer, S. (2009). Attitudes towards school self-evaluation. Studies in Educational Evaluation, 35, 21-28.